Social Security Law in Italy

Social Security Law in Italy

Third Edition

Simonetta Renga

This book was originally published as a monograph in the International Encyclopaedia of Laws/Social Security Law.

Founding Editor: Roger Blanpain
General Editor: Frank Hendrickx
Volume Editor: Willy van Eeckhoutte

Wolters Kluwer

Published by:
Kluwer Law International B.V.
PO Box 316
2400 AH Alphen aan den Rijn
The Netherlands
E-mail: lrs-sales@wolterskluwer.com
Website: www.wolterskluwer.com/en/solutions/kluwerlawinternational

Sold and distributed by:
Wolters Kluwer Legal & Regulatory U.S.
7201 McKinney Circle
Frederick, MD 21704
United States of America
E-mail: customer.service@wolterskluwer.com

ISBN 978-94-035-1676-9

e-Book: ISBN 978-94-035-1356-0
web-PDF: ISBN 978-94-035-1366-9

The Author

Dr Simonetta Renga (born 21 August 1960) studied Law at Perugia University, Perugia (1979–1984). Her final dissertation submitted for the Law degree was awarded a special mention for the National Prize Ludovico Barassi of 1984 by the Italian Association for Labour Law and Social Security and *ex aequo* the National Prize Vito Chiantera of 1986 by the Centre of Studies in Labour Law D. Napoletano. In 1986, she was granted a Council of Europe fellowship for legal studies and research on the European Social Charter. She was then awarded a British Government/British Council FCO scholarship and gained her PhD from the University of Bristol, Faculty of Law (1986–1989). In 1992, she became a solicitor at the Appeal Court of Perugia. Afterwards, she was appointed as researcher at the Chair of Labour Law at Perugia University, Law Faculty (1991–2000). In 1996, she was a visiting scholar at the Wharton School of the University of Pennsylvania with a National Council for Research (CNR) scholarship. In 1998, she was called to take part as an adjunct expert in the governmental commission of experts for the re-ordination of the pension legislation. She took part as a national expert in a study on gender aspects and discrimination with regard to social protection (2009) and in a study on feasibility and added value of a European unemployment benefit scheme (2015), both financed by the European Commission. She was Director of the Department of Economics and Management at Ferrara University from 2010 to 2018. In 2020–2021, she was called to the governmental commission of experts for the reform of unemployment benefits. At present, she is Professor of Labour Law at the Faculty of Economics and Management of Ferrara University, Professor of Social Security Legislation at the Faculty of Law and professor in the Doctoral Course (PhD) in European Union and national legislation at the Faculty of Law. Since 2008, she has been a national expert in the European Commission's Network of legal experts on gender equality. She is the author of a number of books and articles, in Italy and abroad, particularly in the fields of social security law, equal opportunities legislation, and non-standard working patterns.

The Author

Table of Contents

List of Abbreviations

ANPAL	National Agency for Active Labour Policies
ASL/AUSL	Local Health Unities
CIG-CIGS	Short-Time Earning Funds
CIV	Council for Planning and Control
COVIP	Pension Fund Supervisory Committee
DIS-COLL	Unemployment Benefit for 'Para-Employees'
DURC	Certificate of Regular Contributions
ENASARCO	Social Welfare Fund for Representatives and Commercial Travellers
ENPAB	Social Welfare Fund for Biologists
ENPACL	Social Welfare Fund for Consultants
ENPAF	Social Welfare Fund for Pharmacists
ENPAIA	Social Welfare Fund for Farm Managers and Labourers
ENPAM	Social Welfare Fund for Doctors and Dentists
ENPAV	Social Welfare Fund for Veterinary Surgeons
EPPI	Social Welfare Fund for Industrial Experts
FIS	Fund for Salary Integration
GDP	Gross Domestic Product
GOL	Guarantee for Workers Employability
GP	General Practitioners
INAIL	National Institute for Social Insurance Against Industrial Accidents and Occupational Diseases
INPDAP	National Institute of Social Security and Assistance for Public Administration Employees
INPGI	Social Welfare Fund for Journalists
INPS	National Social Welfare Institute
IRPEF	Personal Income Tax
ISCRO	Extraordinary Income and Operating Continuity Allowance
ISEE	Equivalent Economic Situation Indicator
ISTAT	National Institute of Statistics
LEA	Uniform Levels of Assistance

List of Abbreviations

NASPI	Unemployment Benefit Scheme
NHS	National Health Service
PNRR	National Recovery and Resilience Plan
RDC	Citizenship Income
RITA	Integrative Temporary Pension
SINP	National Informative Service for Prevention of Accidents at the Workplace

General Introduction

§1. General Background

1. The Italian social security system envisaged by the Constitution is essentially based on Article 38, Article 3, paragraph 2 and Article 2. Article 38 states: 'Every citizen who is unable to work and who has not sufficient means to live on shall have the right to maintenance and social assistance. Workers shall have the right to adequate protection in relation to their necessities in cases of accidents, sickness, invalidity, old age, and involuntary unemployment. Invalids and the disabled shall have the right to a proper education and to professional starting off schemes. Bodies or institutes set up or integrated by the State shall provide for the above. Private assistance is free.' Article 3, paragraph 2 says: 'The Republic shall remove all social and economic obstacles which actually limit the freedoms and equality of the citizens and consequently prevent a full individual progress as well as the effective participation of workers to the political, social, and economic organization of the Country.' Article 3, paragraph 2 is a complement to Article 2, which says, 'The Republic […] requires the observance of the duties of political, economic, and social solidarity.'

The social security project provided for by our Constitution has been interpreted in different ways, helped by the fact that Article 38 of the Chart is not entirely clear on the matter. Article 38, in fact, speaks of 'citizens unable to work' in paragraph 1 and of 'workers' in paragraph 2: this unhappy wording has left room for the configuration of different social protection instruments for the two categories. Article 38 has given rise to different interpretations of the social security model sanctioned by the Constitution: one theory says that a distinction must be made between assistance and social insurance, the first being for citizens in a state of need and the second for workers struck by certain events; whereas another theory insists upon the entirety of the social protection system; the most recent theory, finally, postulates that Article 38 is neutral on the question of the alternative between assistance and social insurance. The theoretical conflict touches the very roots of the system by questioning the implementing instruments and, therefore, the essential characteristics of guaranteed care. In addition, many benefits ambiguities in Italy are caused by the intermittent implementation of the constitutional norms and by the stratification of benefits laws in different historical periods. In particular, lawmakers have not always followed a consistent and constant project when drafting bills but have often operated on the basis of contingent and contradictory policies. As far as the sources of social protection are concerned, their heterogeneous nature is caused by the fact that the laws governing the social security system were passed in different historical periods, when the conceptions of the role of the state were heavily coloured at a political level. One needs only to remember that in our present-day legislation there still are norms from the Liberal and Fascist periods.

2. The father of the dualistic theory, that is, the theory that postulates a separation between assistance and social insurance, is Alibrandi.[1] This scholar is convinced that Article 38, paragraph 1, was meant to deal exclusively with the citizens in condition of need: assistance provided for them – something less than the insurance protection provided for workers – is completely financed by central government funds. Paragraph 2, on the other hand, deals with workers through social insurance: the material scope of social protection is limited to the events specified by law; the schemes are financed with the cooperation of the relevant workers. There is thus a close correlation between coverage and the worker's professional status and between salary and contributions. According to Alibrandi's theory, the current Italian system is the result of an integration between social insurance and assistance.

3. The universalistic theory is proposed by Persiani.[2] According to him, the model of social security proposed by the writers of the Italian Constitution is seen in a unitary public service destined to free all citizens – including workers – from need, according to the principle of substantial equality; the costs of this are borne by the central government.

Persiani says:

> Of course, Article 38 of the Constitution distinguishes between citizens and workers, but distinguishing is not the same thing as differentiating. Also, if we give the due relevance to the fact that the State intervention to remove the situations of need has become a general interest (Article 3, paragraph 2, Constitution), and is, at the same time, a specific human right as it guarantees the conditions to enjoy basic fundamental rights, we must admit that the State intervention must concern workers and citizens alike. In this light, the distinction between assistance and social insurance can only be brought down to differences in scale and scope, with no basic justification other than the different way in which various laws have considered the needs of citizens compared with those of workers. The named distinction does not rest upon a different foundation.[3]

The same writer, in harmony with the social security plan sanctioned by the Constitution, reconstructs the relationships existing in the ambit of social insurance, between employers, workers, and benefit agencies in terms of autonomous relations: on the one hand, there exists a relation between the employer and the benefit agency ('contributory relationship'); on the other hand, there exists a relation

1. G. Alibrandi, *Infortuni sul lavoro e malattie professionali* (Milan: Giuffré, 1979).
2. M. Persiani, *Diritto della previdenza sociale* (Padua: Cedam, 1988).
3. M. Persiani, *Diritto della previdenza sociale* (Padua: Cedam, 1988), 26–27.

between the benefit agency and the worker (the so-called social insurance relationship). He stresses by these distinctions the fact that the 'contributory relationship' and the 'social insurance relationship' are functional to the public objectives of social protection.[4] Alibrandi's insurance conception of social protection, in contrast, drafted the relationships between the various parties of the social protection system as a trilateral relationship, where the employer insures, the worker is insured, and the agency is the insurer.

4. According to the latest doctrinal interpretation of the Italian social security system, the Constitution model sought is open to interpretation. Cinelli[5] says that the Constitution does not lay down any particular social security model; it does not specify what tools should be used to reach social protection goals.[6] The writer steers well clear of giving a definition of the very concept of social security, saying he finds it too generic. He agrees that the Constitution did seek social security, but quotes as actual the postulate according to which 'the term "social security" does not indicate any legally-defined category but is, in the present day language, a way of encapsulating social and legal experiences which must be heterogeneous and changeable, although they have the final aim of delivering social protection to people in terms of their fundamental individual and common needs'. He, therefore, proposes a definition of the boundaries of the social protection system based upon the 'specific structures and methods' used to deal with socially important negative events. In particular, he points out that 'the subject being dealt with here is indeed an expression of the principle of solidarity and of promotion of the individual, but nevertheless it does not necessarily cover every activity those principles touch upon and which they try to foster'. Rather, 'the element which distinguishes and qualifies the matter here dealt with can be seen [...] in the imposition of rules and instruments designed precisely for the purpose of social protection. And among these, the most important is social insurance, that is the element which, from a practical point of view, coalesce all the others and define them'.[7] Although Cinelli then goes on to admit that if social insurance is taken as the defining factor in the social protection system, there are also instruments of protection of citizens in condition of need or healthcare provisions or instruments of protection of non-productive activities (for those who look after a relative, for example), which cannot then be easily collocated.[8]

5. In this study, we accede to the universalistic theory of social security. The evident contradictions of Article 38 do not mean we cannot integrate Article with the constitutional principles set out in Articles 3, paragraph 2, and 2: according to this interpretation, the social security system can be seen as a set of regulations that require the central government, that is, the general solidarity, to pay for goods and

4. M. Persiani, *Diritto della previdenza sociale* (Padua: Cedam, 1988), Chs II–IV.
5. M. Cinelli, *Problemi di diritto della previdenza sociale* (Turin: Giappichelli, 1989). *See also* M. Cinelli, *Diritto della previdenza sociale* (Turin: Giappichelli, 2001).
6. The author has found confirmation of the open nature of the benefits system foreseen by the Italian Constitution in Decision of the Constitutional Court No. 31 of 1986.
7. M. Cinelli, *Diritto della previdenza sociale* (Turin: Giappichelli, 2001), 8–11.
8. M. Cinelli, *Diritto della previdenza sociale* (Turin: Giappichelli, 2001), 8–11. *See also* 15–17.

services for needy citizens in order that they can take an active part in the economic, political, and social life of the country.[9] The structures of the various instruments geared to implement the social security system depend on the type of cause of distress. Articles 38, 3, paragraph 2 and 2 of the Constitution require services to be functional, not only in removing the negative effects of a situation of distress but also in removing the cause of a state of need. Only direct action against the causes of distress, where this is possible, can guarantee the complete reinstatement into the society of the person in need and the effective exercise of civil and political rights that this entails. It is obviously clear that if the aim of a system is the removal of situations that cause need, then it is vital that a sort of specialization in the social security system be based on the characteristic of the various causes of need. An example of this can be found in disease-care institutes. The care they provide is both economical and medical: the first deals with the earnings-related consequences of the illness; the second is involved with the prevention, care, and rehabilitation in favour of the applicant with health problems, that is to say, with removing the cause of distress.[10] Incidentally, it is worth pointing out that the differentiation of services according to the particular situation of distress involved is not in contrast with a basic uniformity of coverage for all needy citizens, as the Italian Constitution requires. The people covered by the system are indeed the needy citizens, and the type of aid they can apply for depends on the situation of distress they find themselves in, such as unemployment, or sickness, or invalidity, the removal of which is the principal aim of the social protection system. Financial services, upon which applicants also depend for their reintegration into society, are patently insufficient for the removal of the cause of the distress. On the other hand, to link the services issued to the nature of the causes of distress does not mean to limit the social protection only to a legally specified situation: the aim of social protection is first and foremost to deal with situations of need, whatever has caused them; dedicating a service to a particular situation of distress would only mean varying the services provided according to the different nature of the cause of need, naturally maintaining in all the situations the basic economic aid guaranteed by Article 38 of the Italian Constitution.

§2. Historical Background

6. The first sort of social security to be seen in Italy was provided by the Mutual Aid Societies. These associations were set up around the middle of the nineteenth century, and Act No. 3818 was passed in 1886 to deal with them. They were voluntary associations of workers and provided insurance-type coverage but without insurance companies: in this way they shared common risks (sickness, accidents,

9. *See*, more specifically, M. Persiani, *Diritto della previdenza sociale* (Padua: Cedam, 1988), 25 et seq.; and the *Commentario della Costituzione* cured by G. Branca (Zanichelli – Il Foro italiano, Bologna and Rome, 1979) sub-Art. 38; and G. G. Balandi, *Per una definizione del diritto della previdenza sociale*, in *Politica del diritto*, 1984, 576.
10. Articles 32 and 38, Constitution; Act No. 833 of 1978. *See also* M. Cinelli, *La tutela del lavoratore contro la disoccupazione* (Milan: Angeli, 1982), 249–250.

disability, unemployment, death, etc.) within their communities. The Italian government was in those days very favourable towards Mutual Aid Societies. The Mutual Aid Societies hit hard times for a series of reasons, which were connatural to this form of social protection. First of all, only the better-off workers could take part, and so, only a relatively limited number of people were covered. Thus the societies could never reach a situation of having adequate funds. Furthermore, members were never sufficiently expert in company management and carrying out actuarial calculations.

7. The first time the state intervened in benefit matters was with Act No. 80, passed on 17 March 1898, obliging employers in industry to insure themselves and their employees for accidents. The decision to pass this law was made for several reasons: first, the number of workplace accidents was worryingly high; second, just as in other European countries, there was the need to preserve social order in the face of dangerous and unhealthy working conditions; and, finally, the Mutual Aid Societies were a phenomenon that needed to be controlled by the central authority. The insurance-type method was not chosen accidentally: it followed the experience of the Germans. Actuarial calculations showed that this was the safest way of running aid schemes, thereby allowing budget planning and a reduction of the financial risks typical of insurance contracts. Furthermore, insurance meant that the relevant work categories could take part in the financing of the schemes, which, as well as being an economic advantage, kept benefit provisions within the rules of the market. In Italy, the concept of 'professional risk' was used in order to make the setting up of insurance against workplace accidents politically acceptable. Professional risk is a way of attributing civil responsibility as an alternative to the traditional one based on the concepts of guilty parties and malice aforethought: it also makes those who obtain the most benefit from certain types of economic activity responsible for any damages it causes. Using this method, employers were made responsible not only for any damages caused directly by them but also for those suffered by the employees at work due to their own neglect or Acts of God. The employer's obligations were, however, reduced to signing an insurance contract and paying the premiums. In substance, the employer was relieved of responsibility for damages due to the application of the criterion of professional risk: so the actual value of this type of responsibility was greatly reduced, and the criterion of professional risk turned out to be more than ever a conceptual expedient. Professional risk is not positively dealt with under Italian legislation. However, it is the reason why it has come about that workplace accidents are a necessary and inevitable price to be paid for running businesses profitably. Only more than half a century later this idea would give way to the first timid steps towards accident prevention. Furthermore, it is from the idea of professional risk that the transactive solution was adopted within the insurance against workplace accidents: employers pay the premium and take on the risk of Acts of God, whereas workers – in exchange for a wider coverage – have to accept only partial recompense for their damages. This characteristic is still in force today, as we shall see further on, in modern workplace accident insurance.

8. The most important developments in social protection were brought in under the Liberal government period, that is to say, in the early twentieth century. During that period, the National Fund for workers' old-age and invalidity was set up, first as an optional insurance (Act No. 350, 1898), which later became compulsory and widened to cover other categories (1919). Also during this period, insurance against workplace accidents was improved and widened to cover farm labourers (1917), while maternity and unemployment benefits were introduced (1910 and 1919, respectively). During these years fundamental principles began to be applied, such as the automatic requirement for workers to be covered by social protection, and the state's involvement in financing benefits.

9. The Fascist regime maintained and improved the benefit system set up by the Liberals. The main worry during that time was again the maintenance of law and order. Naturally enough, the state interest in the benefits area passed under the aegis of the Fascist Corporations' solidarity between members of the same group or category and between employers and workers. This was the best way to widen insurance-type benefits, and it helped to keep state financing of schemes to a minimum. During the twenty years of Fascism, compulsory insurance against tuberculosis was introduced (1927), the coverage of insurance against workplace accidents was widened to include occupational diseases (1929), and the insurance against common illnesses was set up (1943). In 1933, the 'Fascist National Institute for Social Insurance' was set up. In 1935, accidents and pensions law were reformed, as was that on unemployment. The 1942 Civil Code sanctioned a general provision: the 'principle of automatic payment of benefits', which grants the payment of benefits to workers even when there has been an employer's failure to pay contributions (Article 2116). This principle had already been introduced with the 1935 reforms of the accidents at work insurance. In the same period, benefit coverage was extended to categories of self-employed workers.

10. A new period in the workers' social protection came, as in many other European countries, after World War II. Indeed, the idea of social security was developed in that period. 'Social security' is a term used to describe the state services for citizens in need so they can enjoy their civil and political rights fully. To be free from poverty thus becomes a social right. The main plank in the social security system is the extension of social protection to all citizens in condition of need, whatever the causes of need are. This replaced the older systems exclusively based on insurance. Social insurance grants limited protection as regards both the situations of need and the personal scope of application of the schemes; moreover, social protection is granted through the financial cooperation of the persons covered by the schemes. The idea of social security implies the evolution from care for a restricted category of people – typical of insurance – to a system based on general solidarity: the implementation of a social security system is granted by the whole community organized as a state. Under the Italian Constitution, as we shall see later on, these principles are mentioned in the following articles: in Article 38, specifically targeted to social protection; in Article 3, paragraph 2, which provides for the principles of substantial equality; in Article 2, which sanctions the duty of social solidarity; in Article 32 on healthcare. The welfare system described in Articles 38 and 32 of the Constitution is closely linked to the principles of substantial equality sanctioned by Article 3, paragraph 2: the idea is to provide for a gradual equality of citizens by removing economic and social obstacles that prevent a full individual progress as well as the effective participation of workers in the political, social, and economic life of the country. All the citizens are called upon to implement this project, not merely the state: indeed, Article 2 requires that people assume their duties in terms of political, social, and economic solidarity.

11. The social security project contained in the Italian Constitution has not always meant that legislation on this matter has been fully coherent with its guiding principles. Legislators have not always passed laws according to a well-thought-out plan and have often looked more closely for answers to contingent problems. In the overall body of Italian laws on social protection, however, there are some basic institutions that are rooted in the constitutional plan for social security. In particular, we may point out: the setting up, in 1965, of the Social Fund (which was taken over in 1988 by the Social Assistance Fund run by the National Institute for Social Protection (INPS)), which paid a quota of basic pensions, the integration to the minimum of pensions and the social pension; the social pensions to over-65s without income, launched in 1965 and now covered by the social allowance introduced with the 1995 reform; the raising of all pensions to the legal minimum limits, which was abolished under the 1995 reform; civil invalidity benefit, launched in 1971; the setting up of the National Health Service (NHS) in 1978 for all the citizens and paid for by the state. The principles of welfare have also permeated other solutions adopted by Parliament, such as: the choice, for example, of the system based on distribution rather than that based on capitalization in the management of the public pensions funds (this decision is still in place, even after the 1995 reform); the widening of social protection to cover not only those under a contract of employment but also the self-employed and care workers; the 'principle of automatic payment of benefits', according to which benefits are paid even when the employer has not paid the contributions to the fund (this principle has recently been strengthened in the hypothesis of employers' insolvency). On the other hand, the system has never completely abandoned the insurance principles, even during the late 1960s and early 1970s, when Italy came very close to having a proper social security system. This can be seen by looking at the social insurance against industrial accidents and occupational disease, where there has always been a link between risk and contributions levels, to give merely one example; or in unemployment insurance, where the technical concept of risk conditions both the subjective and objective areas of coverage.

12. From the second half of the 1970s onwards, in Italy, as in most parts of the West, the whole idea of a Welfare State began to be questioned, at the same time as public finances entered into a period of crisis. One of the positive effects of the crisis was the abolition of many excessive care provisions: this state was reached with the harmonization of many different pension schemes. Another effect was the introduction of means testing, that is, the measurement of the beneficiary's earnings when deciding whether to pay him/her benefits. The tendency has been to consider real – and not merely presumed – needs by taking into account the family's income. For example, strict earnings limits are applied when calculating minimum pensions, invalidity benefit, and family income support. Very recently, as we shall see further on, 'earning situation indicators' have been worked out, and these are used in considering applications for social assistance benefits. From 1978 to 1992, many attempts were made at reforming the whole system, none of which worked out, in order to stem the outflow of cash from the system. In 1992 a widespread attempt at reforming the pension system was started, and it ended with the 1995 reform. The most important laws on social security enacted before the 1990s were as follows:

- the equalization (always downwards) of the various mechanisms used to link pensions to the cost of living;
- the reform of family income support;
- the introduction of charges for using the National Health system;
- the reform of the pensions system for the self-employed;
- the abolition of early pensions for civil servants after fourteen years, six months, and one day of contributions payments (the so-called baby pensions);
- the simplification of the administrative organization of the pensions system by definitely entrusting INPS with the management of the private sector, including the area of self-employment, and INPDAP (National institute of social security and assistance for public administration employees) with the management of the public sector;
- the separation, within INPS, of assistance provisions from contributory schemes.

13. The rationalizing and harmonizing of the contributory system undertaken in the 1980s continued with the 1992 reforms.[11] This legislation was passed in an attempt to reduce public expenditure on pensions and was necessary due to economic conditions. In particular, the 1992 legislation deals with:

- the widening of the period taken into account to define the amount of earnings to be taken into consideration in calculating the pension;
- the gradual raising of the retirement age;
- the increase of the minimum amount of contributions that have to be paid in for old-age pensions;
- the introduction of the system of private pension schemes;
- the narrowing of the gap between pensions for the Civil Service and the private sector.

14. Under these principles also comes the pension reform passed in 1995 with Act No. 335. The main aims of this law were to balance the budget and harmonize the various pension schemes. The sword of Damocles of finance problems also hangs over this law. The main changes introduced with the law are the following:

- the move away from a pay-back system when calculating pensions, based on what the applicant's salary was, to a contributory one, based on how many contributions have been paid in over the years;
- the introduction of a flexible pension age;

11. Act No. 421 of 1992; Law Decree No. 503 of 1992.

- the introduction of a more rigorous discipline of the retirement pensions, which will be absorbed in a few years' time into the reformed old-age pension;
- a stabilizing of pensions expenditure, in rigorous accordance with the trends in the gross domestic product (GDP) and its variations;
- the harmonization between the various pension systems;
- an improvement in additional, private pension schemes as a backup to the public one.

As has already been pointed out,[12] what is really new about this reform, more than the re-introduction of the contributory system in calculating pensions, is the linking of both pension calculations and level of contributions to the GDP, that is, to the country's earnings. An extremely important aspect of the new reality is the importance given to private additional pension schemes: these are also promoted through tax relief on the contributions paid to the private funds. Given the constant difficulties Italian governments have faced in maintaining public expenditure, the presence of another pillar is vital in keeping pensions at an acceptable level, and this also frees up money for investments. In the same way, the system has been enriched with a third pillar, whereby private individuals can sign up for their own pension plans offered by an insurance company or pay into private 'open pension funds'. The political choice of favouring private funds has over time been widened to cover health benefits additional to the NHS provisions. The legislator, during the last decade of the twentieth century, has completely reformed the discipline of complementary funds with the target of expanding them and favouring the workers' subscription to them.

The reforms of the period from 1992 to 1995 had objectives of medium and long time well defined: the financial stability of the system, its harmonization, and a higher level of equity. Given these objectives, the legislator enacts a coherent whole of provisions and principles. In the following years, the legislative development is characterized, on the other hand, by the continuous research of immediate savings, regardless of eventual incoherencies introduced in the system. This trend is made clear, over and above but not only, by the pension legislation. Indeed, the 1995 reform provided for an extremely long transitory period before its full coming into force: this was determined by the necessity of granting to workers their acquired rights as well as their mere expectations. This has caused, however, a postponement of the functioning of the mechanisms of financial re-equilibrium and, consequently, new instruments for an immediate saving of resources had to be devised. In this context can be explained the limits imposed on the aggregation of contributions and the constant increase of contributions rates. The need to save resources also inspired the so-called windows intervention, according to which the start of the years-of-service pension was fixed by predetermined dates in the year, which were differentiated in relation to the moment when the qualifying conditions were fulfilled. This might cause up to a one-year postponement in the payment of the pension. The attempt was at discouraging workers to use years-of-service pensions in order to increase the medium age of retirement, which is particularly low in Italy. The main problem of the provisions just described rests on the fragmentation of the discipline, which

12. M. Cinelli, *Diritto della previdenza sociale* (Turin: Giappichelli, 2001), 55.

has become really difficult to read, and on the loss of coherence in relation to the original planning. The attention paid, during these years, by the legislator to the pensions system left aside other problems of our social security system, which are nevertheless important. Thus, among others, nothing has been done to improve the social protection of those who never managed to enter the labour market.

15. At present, the fundamental challenges that the Welfare State is facing are: introduction of active security, social integration, conservation of the linkage between social protection and work, maintenance of non-standard work in the area of social security.

In the attempt to adapt the social security system to the changing socio-economics situation, the legislator has: progressively enhanced the pensionable age; tried to reduce expenses; shifted social protection from the public to the private funds. Therefore, the flexible pensionable age provided by Act No. 335/1995 was replaced by a fixed, higher pensionable age, which is now biannually adjusted to the increase of the average life expectancy;[13] the years-of-service pension was abolished; the transformation coefficients of the individual contribution total were modified so as to reduce the pension amount. Act No. 214/2011, in particular, had the objective of strengthening the sustainability over time of the pensions system in terms of incidence of the social protection expenses on the GDP. This piece of legislation generalized the contribution system criteria of pension calculation for all contributions matured since 1 January 2012 onwards. Moreover, several solidarity contributions were introduced, the automatic equalization was reduced and the costs of unification of national insurance periods were increased. On the other hand, it was impossible to reduce the expenses for the social protection of the unemployed, given the high unemployment rates; furthermore, we still have a disorganized, piecemeal approach to this area of legislation. In particular, we witnessed the misuse of short-time earning funds managed at a local level. The most incisive exercise geared to a rationalization of the social protection measures for the unemployed was realized through Legislative Decree No. 22/2015 and Legislative Decree No. 148/2015, implementing Act No. 183/2014.[14] Finally, often the unemployment benefits were paid within the limits of the sums earmarked to this purpose and this in turn has weakened the nature of individual rights of the benefit perceived.

In this context, there was a shift of resources in the area of occupational funds through the use of the employees' severance allowance (a form of deferred payment). Occupational funds have also taken care, since 2012, of paying short-time earning allowances to those workers who are not included in the public system of protection against temporary working time reductions. Supplementary occupational social security was developed in the area of healthcare, as well.

The present-day social security system has also been influenced by the policy of federalism on public financing: in particular, the reform of Article 117 of the Constitution devolved occupational and supplementary social security to the legislative competence of regions and confirmed, however, the exclusive competence of the state over both public social security and the definition of the minimum benefits

13. Act No. 243/2004, Act No. 247/2007, Act No. 102/2009, Act No. 214/2011.
14. *See also* Act No. 92/2012.

level. Finally, the social security system is strongly conditioned by the constitutionalization of the European Union budgetary constraints contained in the Fiscal Compact and embodied in Article 81 of the Italian Constitution.

§3. Sources of the Social Security System

16. Under the Italian legislation, social protection rights are guaranteed, in the first place, by the Constitution. They are fundamental social rights, the implementation of which is entrusted to Parliament. In particular, Article 38, paragraph 1 states, 'every citizen who is unable to work and who has not sufficient means to live on shall have the right to maintenance and social assistance'. Paragraph 2 goes on to say, 'workers shall have the right to adequate protection in relation to their necessities in cases of accidents, sickness, invalidity, old age, and involuntary unemployment'. Still with Article 38, it says, 'invalids and the disabled shall have the right to a proper education and to professional starting off schemes'. The article also states that 'bodies or institutes set up or integrated by the state' shall provide for the above. Finally, Article 38 says that 'private assistance is free'. Article 32 of the Constitution, on the other hand, says, 'The Republic regards health care as a basic human right and one of society's interests, and guarantees free care for the needy.' These norms must be read together with Article 3, paragraph 2. Taken together, they codify a fundamental principle of the Constitution: the principle of substantial equality. Article 3 says: 'The Republic shall remove all social and economic obstacles which actually limit the freedoms and equality of the citizens and consequently prevent a full individual progress as well as the effective participation of workers to the political, social, and economic organization of the Country.' Article 3, paragraph 2 is a complement to Article 2, which says, 'The Republic [...] requires the observance of the duties of political, economic, and social solidarity.' In Italy's system, therefore, freedom from want is qualified and worked out in connection with the principle of substantial equality: the final objective is full human development. All the citizens are called upon to take part in the welfare project, as well as the state, in compliance with the solidarity duties imposed by Article 2.

17. Paragraph 2 of Article 38 of the Constitution, which deals with workers, makes certain events relevant: accidents at work, sickness, invalidity, old age, and involuntary unemployment. It must be said that this list is open to additions: for example, death, which is covered in the system by survivors' pensions, is not mentioned. Other benefits, not mentioned in the Constitution but which have legal status, are family income support schemes and those concerned with care workers. Article 38 guarantees workers 'adequate means for their needs'. Benefits must therefore satisfy the needs of a worker and his/her family. For applicants, a subjective and perfect right is recognized, which cannot be renounced or disposed of. The most difficult problem in this area is deciding what is meant by 'adequate means'. Under the term 'means', as well as money, must surely come services provided by the various benefits agencies (such as medical and preventative care provided by the NHS). The very concept of adequate means is ambiguous in itself. It might mean a basic equal minimum level or the preservation of the worker's way of living. The problem, therefore, is attempting to see where the social protection envisaged by the Constitution places it between these two extremes. Parliament has always tried to face the problem realistically. The benefits system has often tended to maintain the level of earnings reached by the applicant: one need only think of the pensions calculations that were used until the 1995 reforms. In other areas, basic constitutional guarantees have been violated: for example, actual minimum pension levels are extremely low. When deciding benefit levels, Parliament often made contingent economic considerations, such as public finance crises or high unemployment levels. The 1995 pension reform is of particular importance here, as benefit spending was linked to GDP, and thereby providing some indication of the resources available.[15]

18. The insertion of social protection rights into the Italian Constitution has more than once required an intervention of the Constitutional Court. Scholars affirmed that 'the dialectic relationship between Constitutional Court and Parliament [...] has been extremely important in this area, and especially in recent times'; the Court is seen as 'an important factor of dynamism for the whole benefits system'.[16] The Court has made decisions based on both the principle of equality stated in Article 3 and the provisions of Article 38. Starting from the equality principle, the scope of insurance has often been widened and a right to the most favourable retirement treatment has been recognized. On the other hand, unjustifiable inequalities have been eliminated by removing privileges in certain categories. Often, especially when dealing with the aggregation rules of minimum basic pensions, there has been a real conflict of interests between political decisions adopted to safeguard the economic balance of the system and decisions taken by the Constitutional Court in favour of claimants. This phenomenon has always been worse when the economy has been in a crisis. Following decisions made by the Constitutional Court, Parliament has often had to pass laws to sort out the imbalance introduced. But recently, the Court itself has taken decisions based on a more rigorous economic discipline. Less frequent have been the decisions made concerning Article 38. When dealing with this area, the Court has often stated the difference between the assistance and the contributory schemes, has decided on the question of 'adequate means' as being those required to maintain the applicant in the style of life to which he/she has become accustomed, and has stated that pensions must be proportional to the contributions paid in. It has also stated that benefits must be index-linked, and that retroactive laws are prejudicial to citizens' confidence in their social protection rights.[17]

19. The social security system is regulated by an articulated and complex body of Acts of Parliament. Many rules have been passed in order to reduce public expenditure and have been inserted into the annual Finance Bill. As well as these, there have been passed a series of legislative decrees, decree laws, and administrative

15. *See* on the matter M. Cinelli, *Diritto della previdenza sociale* (Turin: Giappichelli, 2001), 145 et seq.
16. M. Cinelli, *Diritto della previdenza sociale* (Turin: Giappichelli, 2001), 66.
17. For more of these decisions, *see* M. Cinelli, *Diritto della previdenza sociale* (Turin: Giappichelli, 2001), 66 et seq.

regulations, which show how important the role of government has become in this area. However, the Constitutional Court has decided against using decree law as a means of passing urgent laws.[18] Some parts of the legal framework come down from the first decades of the last century.[19] Some parts are contained in the Civil Code, among which we may remind: the principle of automatic payment of benefit (covered by Article 2116); the employer's and employee's requirements to contribute to financing the system (Article 2115); the rule according to which private pension funds are bound to their scope of providing social protection and cannot be used by the employer for private purposes (Article 2117). It is a common opinion, however, that laws passed before the Constitution coming into force must be interpreted in the light of the latter.

20. The state has an exclusive competence in the area of social protection. The regions have legislative competence on healthcare, private additional pensions, and workplace safety. Parliament keeps, however, in these matters the competence to define the general fundamental principles to be applied by the regions. Anyway, Parliament can always hand over special law-making powers to Regions.

21. The pension bodies can make regulations with various degrees of legal force. Some of them can make executive regulations; others can pass decisions concerning contributions; finally, other bodies have a wide financial and regulatory autonomy. Moreover, Act No. 48 passed in 1988 allows the public administration to make decrees or decisions that modify the legislation concerning management structures, contributions, the paying out of benefits, and the contributions rebates for employers.

18. Constitutional Court No. 360 of 1996.
19. *See e.g.*, Royal Decree No. 1422 of 1924; Royal Decree No. 1827 of 1935; Royal Decree No. 636 of 1939.

Part I. The Institutions

Chapter 1. Public Institutions

22. Under Italian law, central government and local authorities (Article 117 Constitution) are responsible for assistance and social insurance. The state may allow private bodies to run these services. But in this case, the agencies involved must follow a series of regulations, which continue to give the state a certain amount of control.

Private companies play only a marginal role in additional schemes, but this is destined to increase with time.

The whole structure of the social security system is extremely complex, some functions being covered by public agencies, others by special bodies.

The main state bodies that play an active part in social protection management are the Employment and Social Policy Ministry, the Health Ministry and the Home Office. However, the denominations and attributions of ministries keep continuously changing with changes in government.

The Employment and Social Policy Ministries have general planning functions in the social insurance sphere. It organizes and directs, supervises and controls the various agencies.

The Health Ministry is in charge of health and sanity. As we shall see, most of its functions have been spread out to the regions, which are in charge of hospitals, general healthcare, and health and safety at work.

Under the Home Office comes the Civil Service Department, which is in charge of the extraordinary social assistance interventions, the care of disabled, and refugees. The Home Office also takes care of international social assistance.

A special Parliamentary Commission supervises the activities of the various social insurance agencies. This activity is complementary to the activity of control reserved for the Employment and Social Policy Ministry and its various branches.

23. The social protection agencies' administrative organization is twofold: some agencies are organized at the institutional level; others are associations.

At the institutional level we find the INPS (*'Istituto Nazionale della Previdenza Sociale'*, or National Social Welfare Institute), which manages the general social insurance system covering compulsory contributory schemes for employees and the special regimes for the self-employed; and again, at an institutional level comes the special regimes for certain types of private-sector workers.

The pension agencies set up as associations include the pension schemes of certain categories of workers, the so-called autonomous or substitutive funds, and the pension funds of self-employed professionals.[20]

The pension agencies set up as associations are normally not subject to the general social insurance regime and tend to provide better services. The agencies are as follows: Social Welfare Fund for freelance Journalists (INPGI);[21] Social Welfare Fund for Representatives and Commercial Travellers (ENASARCO); Social Welfare Fund for Farm Managers and Labourers (ENPAIA). ENASARCO and ENPAIA, however, do not take the place of the general social insurance regime; they merely provide additional services. Contributions to these funds are compulsory.

All the self-employed professionals' Pension Funds, the ENASARCO, the ENPAIA, and the INPGI, have been privatized.[22]

24. In certain cases, basic social protection has been entrusted to company funds especially set up; those who pay into these company funds are exempted from paying into the state funds. These private funds are called 'exonerated funds'. There are also cases where certain companies look after the welfare of their own staff, using the so-called exclusive funds. The exonerated and exclusive funds are authorized to provide coverage only if they can guarantee the same levels as compulsory basic state pensions. They mostly operate in the public sector, the banking sector, and among insurance companies.

25. From the point of view of the situations of distress, there are some specific agencies that cut across various categories of workers. The most important of these is INAIL (National Institute for Social Insurance Against Industrial Accidents and Occupational Diseases), which provides cover for workplace accidents and occupational diseases for most categories of workers.

Finally, social assistance is mainly run by nationwide and regional agencies.

26. Welfare recipients, to a different extent and in different ways, take part in the running of the agencies. Private-sector workers have their trade union representatives, who enjoy the same rights as the employers' representatives, in the Council for Planning and Control (CIV) of INPS and INAIL, where planning and control operations are carried out.[23]

---

20. For these distinctions, *see* M. Cinelli, *Diritto della previdenza sociale* (Turin: Giappichelli, 2018).
21. Article 28, Act No. 234/2021.
22. Law Decree No. 509 of 1994.
23. Act No. 1712/1963, Presidential Decree No. 639/1970, Act No. 88/1989.

Chapter 2. Position and Competence of the Public Institutions

§1. The INPS

27. INPS and INAIL are the two main public welfare agencies. INPS, the National Social Welfare Institute, is in charge of invalidity, old-age and surviving relatives, involuntary unemployment, and tuberculosis benefits. The agency also covers invalidity and old-age individual and collective optional insurance schemes. INPS pays the social allowance to over-67s without earnings, family income support, and the pension to those who do unpaid care work within their families. INPS also runs the short-time earning funds (CIG-CIGS), the mobility allowance, the sickness benefits, and the civil invalidity benefits.

The system run by INPS is general because it tends to cover all regularly employed private and public sector workers, civil servants of the parastatal sector, the self-employed, the associated workers, the precarious workers of the public sector, and all the self-employed professionals who have no special pension funds. Furthermore, the compulsory National Insurance managed by INPS has the function of completing the pensions system as a whole: workers who have been paying into an additional or exonerated scheme and then stop working before reaching the minimum requirements may start a special scheme with INPS whereby the money they paid in elsewhere is counted towards their pensions.

INPS is controlled by the Employment and Social Policy Ministry.

INPS is run on central and peripheral lines (with regional, provincial, and area offices).

INPS has the following structure: the President, who represents the agency legally and runs the agency; the CIV, where the operations of supervision, planning, and control are carried out; the College of Auditors, who supervises the administrative and technical running of the agency; and the Director General.

Alongside these organs are special Committees for each activity undertaken by the agency; these are entrusted with powers of control, appeals, and administrative affairs. Finally, there is the Unified Agricultural Contributions Certification and Collection Commission (*Commissione per l'accertamento e la riscossione dei contributi agricoli unificati*), in charge of farm labourers' social insurance. These Committees operate on a regional and provincial level.

INPS has an inspectorate that has special investigatory powers.

Pursuant to Act No. 88 of 1989, several INPS activities were gathered into special internal funds, which are, however, economically independent, such as:

- the Employees' Pension Fund, which runs compulsory invalidity, old-age, and survivals' social insurance;
- the Employees' Fund for Temporary Benefits, which runs, among others, the unemployment insurance, the tuberculosis insurance, the family income support benefits, the maternity allowance, the sickness pay, the CIG-CIGS, and the mobility allowance;

– the Public Employees' Fund;[24]
– the Agriculture Fund;
– the Traders' and Craft Workers' Fund;
– the Bank Employees' Fund;
– the Self-Employed Fund, called the 'Fourth Fund';
– the Social Assistance and Social Insurance Support Fund, which is financed by the state and runs benefits, the nature of which is totally or partially one of social assistance.

INPS also manages Special Social Insurance Funds for certain categories of workers, some of which are additional and some substitutive in relation to the general compulsory social insurance.

Finally, the INPS runs certain types of social assistance benefits, such as: the social allowance for over sixty-seven citizens, the civil invalidity benefit, maternity allowances, and allowances for low-income families.

INPS also runs bilateral schemes for CIG-CIGS.[25]

§2. The INAIL

28. INAIL, the National Institute for Social Insurance against Employment Accidents and Occupational Diseases (*'Istituto nazionale per le assicurazioni contro gli infortuni sul lavoro e le malattie professionali'*), is in charge of these two areas for industry and agriculture; it also covers those who carry out household and care activities.

The Agency works with both the private and public sectors.

It is both centrally and locally organized, with regional and provincial offices, and has the same organization and structure as INPS.

INAIL also provides assistance benefits to serious workplace accident victims, pays the allowance for those who can no longer work, and pays for prostheses. It carries out medical checks and certifications on the victims of industrial accidents and provides a certain level of first-aid care upon agreements with the local health authorities. INAIL can undertake agreements with the NHS for specialist care for victims of industrial accidents. Finally, INAIL has tasks on workplace accident prevention and takes part, providing for technical and informatics support, in the National Informative Service for Prevention of Accidents at the Workplace (SINP).[26]

---

24. Act No. 214/2011, Art. 21, para. 1, which abolished INPDAP, the former civil servants welfare institute, now incorporated by INPS.
25. *See* Part VII.
26. Article 8, Law Decree No. 81 of 2008.

Chapter 3. Private Institutions

29. Patronage and social assistance institutes are legally set up private associations, which provide free assistance in gaining access to benefits for workers and citizens both in Italy and abroad. They may also represent workers in hearings at the various pensions or benefits agencies, at conciliation boards, and, if so required, in the courts. The Institutes are financed by special funds provided by the Employment and Social Policy Ministry and financed through quotas of the contributions paid to the welfare agencies.

Part II. Contribution and Financing

Chapter 1. Contributions Regulations for Employees and Self-Employed

§1. Field of Application

30. In general, the subjects liable to the payment of obligatory contributions in the sphere of the social security system are: employers, employees, self-employed workers. Occasionally, obligation of contribution may, however, also apply to other subjects: such is the case, for example, of the client of a freelance professional, who has the obligation to contribute to the welfare provision of the professional with a contribution quota related to the value of service received. Normally, in the employment relationship the contributory obligation is shared between workers and employers, who generally pay higher proportions than employees. However, the employer is also responsible for the actual payment of the quota set as incumbent upon the employee. In some cases, however, contributions are exclusively owed by the employer: this occurs, for example, in the case of insurance against industrial accidents and professional diseases.

31. The insurance relationship and the consequent obligation of contribution arise automatically at the moment at which an employment relationship is established, or when someone begins to conduct self-employed work, or when someone joins a professional association or register. In some cases, however, in addition to simply conducting a particular business, it is necessary, for the obligation of contribution to arise, to reach a certain minimum income threshold. This occurs most of all in the sphere of the freelance professions.

32. The existence of an obligation of contribution must be sanctioned by the law, while the total amount of contributions is normally established by the interested welfare bodies with decisions which are then approved by ministerial decrees. At present, only the insurance premiums against industrial accidents and professional diseases are determined in relation to the risk associated with the individual activities covered.

§2. Calculation of Contributions

I. Calculation Base

33. Pay that is taken as the basis for calculation of social security contributions, or the so-called taxable pay, is conventionally established by the law. At present we have in our system two notions of pay taxable for welfare purposes. One is laid down by a law of 1969, which is valid for incomes matured prior to January 1998. This notion was extended to include employees of the public administration, within the general objective of harmonizing the various social security systems, which was pursued by the law on pension reform of 1995. The other, introduced by a law of 1997, is valid for incomes accruing from January 1998 onwards. The new notion of taxable pay, as we shall see, is born of the need to harmonize the criteria for determining welfare taxability with those of fiscal taxability.

34. The law of 1969 considers taxable income as 'all that which the employee receives from the employer in money or in kind, gross of any deduction, dependent upon the employment relationship'.[27] The notion of taxable pay laid down by such a law is all-embracing: virtually any transfer of economic value from employer to worker occurring within the context of their working relationship is considered as pay for social security purposes; thus a direct cause-and-effect relationship with the performance of working activities is not necessary.

35. However, the law lays down a peremptory list of items exempted from tax for social security contribution purposes. In particular, among the items excluded from the taxable base, the following appear: reimbursement of expenses; cash allowances; daily allowances and fixed-sum travel expenses; allowances for employees working off-site or for workers abroad; sums paid as retirement bonus or those paid on the occasion of the termination of a working relationship, which here include those sums paid to encourage early retirement; emoluments for family allowances paid directly by the employer; contributions in the form of secondary pensions, which are subject only to a social solidarity contribution to be paid by the employer; emoluments for canteen services and transport offered by the employer with regard to most workers for needs connected to the activities of work and the relative substitute payments; expenses for climatic camps, for study grants, for kindergartens, and for company clubs and associations. The exemptions from the taxable base, which have gradually increased over time through additional legislation, embrace both the alternative use of resources freed from tax for clearly incentive purposes, and operations to reduce the cost of labour aimed at increasing production and levels of employment. The exemption from the taxable base of contributions to complementary pension funds, for example, is clearly aimed at encouraging the formation of additional forms of social provision to that of the state welfare system.

---

27. Article 12, Act No. 153 of 1969.

Over time, the notion of taxable remuneration has developed more flexibly. The legislator has, indeed, granted the public administration, in this instance the Ministry of Employment, the power to exclude other services (such as those of transport and canteen facilities), which are connected with the activities of work and have a general character for the employees affected, from the taxable base; the Ministry of Employment can establish the said exemption with a decree which is to be issued in concert with the Treasury, once the unions and employers' associations that are most representative on a national level have been consulted.[28] Last, the law[29] has laid down a partial exemption from contribution of payments provided for by collective company contracts, or rather second-level contracts, the payment or totals of which are uncertain and which are designated for measuring increases in productivity, quality, and other elements of competitiveness taken as indicators of the economic progress of the company and its results. In practice, the assisted contribution regime is intended to apply to productivity or incentive wages or bonuses based on results. Such an assisted regime is referred to as 'de-contribution'.

It must, however, be noted that the subtraction of resources from the pension system (which can be effected by means of such instruments), which are available to both the public administration and collective bargaining, carries with it consequences that are more serious in the new pension system introduced by the reform of 1995, compared to the past. The present pension system, indeed, is based, as we shall have the opportunity to appreciate,[30] on a more stringent connection between pension benefits and contribution assets than was the case in the previous system.

36. The legislator, on the other hand, has repeatedly broadened the range of taxable elements to emoluments that are not exactly payments but substitutes for payment, such as: welfare benefits substituting wages; sums paid out to workers by funds, associations, organizations, or forms of insurance recognized by agreements or collective contracts; sums and benefits paid out to workers, even as compensation, for non-fulfilment of obligations accepted with the work contract, or in the context of executive procedures, or following steps taken by the judicial authority; sums received as settlement relative to the termination of a working relationship; and free payments in relation to a working relationship.

37. The notion of taxable remuneration for welfare purposes has then been modified. A law of 1997 laid down that the taxable base for welfare purposes coincides with the income from permanent employment subject to individual income tax.[31] More specifically, the income of permanent employment, which is made up of all sums and benefits in kind – received for any reason during the tax period, even under the form of free donations – is considered taxable for welfare purposes, in relation to the employment relationship. It must be underlined that the criterion of dependence on the employment relationship has become a generic 'in relation to the

28. Article 17, Law Decree No. 503 of 1992.
29. Article 2, Act No. 135 of 1997; Art. 49, Act No. 488 of 1999.
30. *See* Part VIII of this study.
31. Article 6, Law Decree No. 314 of 1997.

employment relationship'. The new notion of taxable remuneration applies in relation to incomes received from January 1998 onwards.

38. The law continues to acknowledge a series of exemptions from the taxable base which, to a great extent, match those accepted by the rule previously in force. Among these are the following: sums paid as retirement bonus or those paid on the occasion of the termination of a working relationship, which here include those sums paid to encourage early retirement; cash allowances; within certain limits, the free payments granted by the employer on the occasion of public holidays or anniversaries to all employees or to categories of workers; meals consumed in company canteens or substitute payments; supply of collective transport; tips for croupiers in casinos. The system of 'de-contribution' also applies in relation to the new notion of taxable remuneration.

39. The contribution of self-employed workers with their own pension system, of self-employed workers who carry out continuative and coordinated collaborations, and of professionals with their own pension fund is calculated on the annual income declared for individual income tax purposes.

40. The law lays down a minimum pay limit to be taken into consideration with a view to calculating welfare contributions owed. The minimum contribution threshold is equal to 9.5% of the minimum monthly pension paid out in the relevant year by the system of obligatory invalidity, old-age and survivors' insurance. Another limit in the calculation of welfare contributions is given by the fact that the remuneration to be considered as the basis for calculation cannot be less than the amount of payments laid down by laws, regulations, and collective contracts stipulated by the main representative national unions. In the case of a range of varying collective contracts for the same category, the one that applies is that stipulated by the union organizations that are comparatively most representative in the category. The remuneration established by an individual contract can only be taken into consideration when it is superior to that laid down by the collective contract.[32] In substance, such provisions no longer take into consideration, for the purposes of calculating contributions, the payment actually paid out; it has become relevant instead to consider the obligatory minimum laid down by the law or by collective contracts, according to Article 36 of the Italian Constitution. In short, defaulting employers, from the point of view of pay levels, are also constrained to pay in welfare contributions on the basis of the remuneration laid down by the law or by collective bargaining.

41. Until 1995, there was no maximum ceiling corresponding to the minimum pay limit to be taken into consideration for contributions. In other words, all income received remained subject to contribution. The 1995 reform, however, established an annual maximum for the contribution base, subject to revaluation by means of

32. Article 1, Act No. 389 of 1989; Art. 2, Act No. 549 of 1995.

the ISTAT (National Institute of Statistics) retail price index. The annual maximum income for contribution is applied as regards the pension calculated according to the contribution system.

II. Contribution Amount

42. Ordinary contribution rates are not the same for all those owing payments. These vary, for example, depending on the nature of the activity of the company: commercial and craft companies pay lower contributions than industrial companies. Other determining factors for the definition of the burden of contribution are: the commodity sector to which the company belongs; the number of employees; the grade of employees (rates for workers are the highest and those for executives the lowest); the location of the company (areas considered depressed have lower contribution rates). There is, in addition, a whole series of reductions in contribution rates as incentives. Such is the case of workers taken on with contracts of apprenticeship or with contracts of solidarity. In the first case the legislator intends to encourage, by means of the contributory instrument, the stipulation of contracts for young people with a training purpose, and more generally youth employment; contracts of solidarity are, on the other hand, instruments for dealing with unemployment.[33] In other cases lower rates are laid down for younger workers or for the long-term unemployed with the aim of encouraging their employment. In other situations, the object of incentives is youth entrepreneurship. Other reductions in contribution rates directed at favouring employment by means of redistribution of work opportunities are planned to the benefit of those who stipulate contracts that make provision for stable reductions in working hours. In other instances, reductions are geared to stimulate forms of pay linked to the improvement of productivity. Lower rates are applied in addition to categories considered weaker, such as: workers employed on domestic and family service; agricultural workers; workers who are members of a cooperative. In other cases, the contribution instrument is used with a penalty function: that is to say, the contributions of those employers who violate certain provisions of the law are increased. Last, the contribution instrument is sometimes used to discourage certain types of behaviour of employers. For example, in all the cases of dismissals due to the employer, he is charged a special contribution.[34]

43. The typology of contributions that reach the funds of the welfare system is vast. Thus, next to obligatory contributions, there are voluntary contributions that are paid in continuation of an obligation that is not in force any longer, with the aim of increasing the individual's own pension. Additional contributions also exist that are paid, as in the case of CIG-CIGS, wholly by the employer who uses a particular welfare benefit. Another type of contribution is that of the social solidarity

33. *See* Part VII of this study in this regard.
34. For greater detail, *see* Part VII of this study.

contributions. Such contributions are paid by certain specific productive categories in the sphere of redistribution policies to the benefit of all or of weaker welfare systems. A contribution of this kind, for example, has been imposed on complementary pension funds to the benefit of the basic public systems.

Chapter 2. Measures of Protection for the Insurance Position of the Worker

§1. The Principles of Aggregation of Income and Unification

44. Various measures exist that are aimed at maintaining the contribution position of a subject when particular events of his/her working life might prejudice it. Among these measures, those that permit periods of insurance contributions that took place under different systems to be considered together as a unit should be mentioned. One of these measures is represented by the principle of aggregation or totalizing of income. This principle allows the subject who might have accrued various contribution periods in several welfare systems to gain a split or pro-rata pension payment from the various systems through a single calculation of the various insurance blocks.

Each portion of the whole pension payment received will be calculated according to the system to which that particular portion refers.

The principle of aggregation is operative in favour of workers who have accrued periods of contributions under various pension schemes and who are not yet entitled to a pension; in order to benefit from the single calculation of the various insurance blocks, however, the worker must be 67 years old and have twenty years' contributions in total, or alternatively, independently from his/her age, man must have at least forty-two years and ten months contributions in total and women at least forty-one years and ten months contributions in total.[35]

45. Another instrument for the preservation of the contribution position is unification. This mechanism is also intended to be to the benefit of those insured persons who are in possession of contribution periods accrued under various welfare bodies. Unification does not expect the simple calculation of the various contribution periods but rather the actual transfer of contributions from one system to another. Thus, the contribution period does not appear in a split form, as occurs in the aggregation system, but is considered as having been accrued entirely under the final contribution system. In this case the whole pension payment is calculated according to the rules of the final system. Generally, the most favourable pension system is chosen. However, it is often necessary to make up a shortfall for the most favourable payment obtained in the chosen system through additional payments by the interested party.

46. Act No. 228/2012 introduced the free aggregation on demand. According to this, each portion of the whole pension payment received will be calculated according to the system to which that particular portion refers, but in the end, the pension will be a unique one, as it happens under the principle of unification; however, the whole operation will not imply any additional payment.[36]

35. Law Decree No. 42/2006; Act No. 247 of 2007; Art. 24, para. 19, Act No. 214/2011. *See also*: Constitutional Court No. 61 of 1999, in Massimario di Giurisprudenza del Lavoro, 1999, 640; Constitutional Court No. 198/2002 and No. 235/2005.
36. Article 1, para. 239, Act No. 228/2012; Art. 1, para. 195, Act No. 236/2016.

§2. Voluntary Continuation, Redemptions, Pension Replenishment, and Pension Supplements

47. In other situations, the law permits the augmentation of the contribution position by making reference to further periods that are additional to those of obligatory contributions. One of the instruments provided by law for this purpose is the voluntary continuation of obligatory insurance. This is authorized, with certain conditions, to an individual who ceases an activity that is subject to obligatory insurance.

48. A further instrument for the improvement of the personal contribution position is that of redemptions. This institution allows additional contributions, referring to periods of working life that did not permit contributions to be made, to come into the individual's pension position. Redemption also serves to integrate contributions paid in periods of reduced pay treatment, as, for example, in the case of part-time work. A classic example of redemption is that of the years of the legally recognized length of a degree course, which has recently been made available also to students not yet registered in any pension scheme.[37] The costs of redemption are to be paid by the interested party.

49. Pension replenishment, on the other hand, is a mechanism that allows the re-calculation of a pension with a view to providing for the counting of periods of professional activity that entailed the right to contribution and which had not been taken into consideration at the moment of settlement of the pension. In short, the right to the re-assessment of the total amount of a pension or its replenishment is acquired when, following its settlement, contributions paid or accrued before the start date of the pension are taken into consideration and counted.

50. Last, supplements to pensions are increases to pensions already being paid that are due to the pensioner who continues to work. These are assessed on the basis of contributions relative to the professional activity carried out by the pensioner and they have a two-year cycle.

§3. The Principle of Automatic Payment of Benefits and the Limitation of Contributions

51. A further instrument aimed at the protection of the pension position of the worker is the principle of automatic payment of benefits. This principle is laid down by Article 2116 of the Civil Code. In compliance with this principle, the benefits to be paid by the obligatory pension and assistance systems are owed to the worker even when the employer has not paid the proper contributions. The principle of automatic payment of benefits naturally applies only to the benefit of the employee and does not extend to the self-employed. In addition, the principle in question applies in a complete manner only for insurance against industrial accidents and

37. Article 1, para. 77, Act No. 247 of 2007.

professional diseases. In the case of obligatory insurance for invalidity, old age, and surviving relatives, the principle only applies within the time period of limitation of contributions. This means that once the employer's debt of contributions is paid off because of statutory limitations, the worker cannot invoke the principle of automatic payment of benefits. Some years ago, however, this principle was strengthened within the pension system as well.[38] In particular, it has been established that in the case of an employer being subject to executive procedure, the worker can ask the welfare institution to consider omitted and prescribed contributions as having been paid. The only condition that the legislator has placed on the applicability of the principle in this case is the previous attempt on the part of the employee to enact proceedings against the employer for redress: the principle will be applicable only if the legal proceedings on the part of the employee have a negative outcome. It must be noted here that the law on pension reform of 1995 unified the limitation term of all contributions to five years. In addition, it must be stated that in the pension field, as a specific dispensation to the general rules, the possibility to regularize contributions in arrears is excluded once the limitation has come into play. This principle, which has the intention of protecting the welfare institutions from unforeseen pension payments, has the effect that once the limitation has come into effect, the contribution position of a worker is definitively prejudiced. There remain available to him/her only, as we shall see, a formal legal application for the establishment of a life annuity, or an action for damages against the employer who did not fulfil his contributory obligation (Article 2116 of the Civil Code).[39]

38. Article 3, Law Decree No. 80 of 1992.
39. *See* Part X of this study.

Chapter 3. Government Funding

§1. Full Payment Out of General Taxation

52. The funding model of the Italian social security system is based on the parallel contribution of the categories involved and state intervention. The intervention of state finance is usually realized first of all through funding, by the state, of the Social Assistance and Social Insurance Support Fund of INPS. The law has placed the benefits directed towards assistance and social ends in the hands of this managing body. In particular, the following are included, among others: social allowances; subsidies of invalidity benefits; minimum pension subsidies; early retirement pensions; social security contribution rebates; CIG-CIGS; special unemployment benefits; economic payments of insurance against tuberculosis. In addition, the state intervenes by means of contributions earmarked to wipe out the deficits of the INPS budget; to such an end that the state contribution is paid annually, on the occasion of the finance act (Budget Act), or with normative interventions designed for specific cases of deficit.

53. The welfare reform of 1995[40] attempted to rationalize and plan state intervention in the pension sphere. In the first place, this reform fixed the contribution rate of pension financing payable by workers at a higher percentage of taxable income, keeping unchanged the overall contribution level. In the second place, the reform granted the annual finance act, prepared by the government and approved by Parliament, the power to modify the estimate rate for calculation of pensions, when this might be necessary to maintain the financial balance of pension administration.

§2. Notional Contributions

54. Another form of state financial intervention in the social security system comes about through notional contribution. Notional contribution is a fictional contribution paid by the state: it substitutes employers' and employees' contributions in specific cases of suspension or termination of their working relationship. The causes for suspension or termination of contract covered by the notional contribution are listed specifically by the law. Among others, let us mention: illness, pregnancy, maternity leave, injury, unemployment, work absence due to the need to assist handicapped relatives, use of parental leave, permitted leave for public or union appointments, annulment of contract for political, religious or union reasons. The object of the notional contribution is to prevent workers from suffering prejudice on the future enjoyment of pension benefits due to events that are socially justified and that have an effect on the continuity of their working relationship. The notional contribution applies to both the total amount of and the right to welfare benefits.

40. Act No. 335 of 1995.

§3. Social Security Contribution Reduction and Relief from Contributions

55. Social security contribution reductions are a measure by which a portion of the obligatory contributions owed by a company for sickness assistance is financed/ paid by the state. These contribution reductions apply to various sectors of production. A provision of this kind clearly results in a reduction in labour costs. The reduction in contribution is determined as a fixed sum, differentiated by the category of worker. The contribution reduction is also subordinate to the payment to employees of affected firms of a pay deal not lower than the minimum laid down by collective agreement. In particular, contribution reductions are granted to those employers falling within the field of application of such a concession, as long as they pay their employees' salaries that are not lower than those laid down by national and provincial collective contracts. In the same way, those employers who inform the welfare agencies of their employees with payments that are lower than those laid down by collective contracts, or with hours or days of work that are lower than those really carried out, are excluded from this allowance. Last, those employers who fail to report the existence of their employees to the welfare agencies are excluded from the allowance. Exclusion from the allowance in these cases also extends beyond the period of non-observance of the above-mentioned obligations, up to a duration of 50% of the period. In areas of high unemployment, however, social security contribution reductions are also recognized for employers who pay their employees' salaries that are lower than those laid down by collective contracts, as long as they commit themselves to bring the payment of their employers back up to the level laid down by collective contract. The operation to re-stabilize wages paid to their employees must occur gradually, by means of collective company contracts that are in conformity with provincial collective contracts of so-called realignment.

In order to get contribution reductions, in general, employers have to obtain the certificate of regular contributions (so-called DURC).[41]

56. Relief from contributions are reduction in contributions owed to the various bodies of the INPS (National Social Welfare Institute) by industrial and craft companies operating in the South of Italy. These concessions were introduced for the first time in 1968 with the aim of favouring the development of industrial activity and the increase of employment in the South of Italy. The financial burden of these reductions in contributions is taken on by the state. The relief is calculated as a percentage of the payments that are subject to the obligation to contribution, net of payments for overtime work. However, various types of relief are laid down, which can also apply jointly, with different criteria of calculation. The reduction is effected materially by means of the mechanism of adjustment between the total amount of contributions owed by the employer and that of the relief. The adjustment occurs monthly, and the total relief cannot exceed that of the contributions owed. Recognition of relief is dependent upon the fact that payments reported to the INPS and

41. Article 1, para. 1175, Act No. 296/2006.

paid to workers are not lower than those laid down by national and provincial collective contracts. The matter of relief has been greatly deregulated, that is to say, the subject has been entrusted to ministerial decrees.[42]

57. Through the mechanisms of social security contribution reductions and relief it is clear that the welfare system is transformed into an instrument of economic policy. Public finance, indeed, takes on financial burdens corresponding to a part of welfare contributions with the aim of advantaging certain productive categories or certain territorial areas that are underdeveloped. The compatibility of these steps, which have the nature of state aids, with the provisions of EU legislation relative to the prohibition against introducing or maintaining measures that may alter the rules of free competition, according to Article 87 of the Treaty, must always be verified. On this subject, the ministerial decrees that will have the task of regulating the matter of relief are obliged to take the trends of the European Union into account. The Commission of the European Union in particular has imposed spending limits beneath which free competition rules (between two parties) will not be considered to have been infringed (so-called *de minimis* rule).

42. Act No. 30 of 1997.

Part III. Healthcare

Chapter 1. The National Health Service

§1. The Objectives of the NHS

58. In 1978, Act No. 833 set up the NHS (*Servizio Sanitario Nazionale*). This law was one of the centre points of Italian Social Security. The NHS became the enactment of Article 32 of the Constitution, which says 'Italy shall protect health as a basic human right and social interest.' In the Constitution, health, therefore, becomes a general value and public interest; health is no longer collocated a merely individual level. The reform meant the suppression of National Institute for Health Insurance, of the mutual sick pay funds, and of the health sectors of other welfare agencies. It provided healthcare for all the citizens, with the same rights for everyone. The reform connected healthcare not only to the curing of diseases but also to their prevention and the rehabilitation of invalids.

59. During the 1990s, many attempts were made at reforming the healthcare service. In particular, this was due to a wide variety of factors, such as the economic crisis of the health sector, efficiency and bureaucracy problems, and the need to rationalize the system. It was said that allowing local authorities' managers to run the system was not a happy choice: the lack of specific qualifications meant that the service was mismanaged. A first series of laws, passed in the early 1990s, shows that Parliament had re-thought the principles of general and universal cover.[43] The most important amendments concern a re-shaping of the benefits universally guaranteed to all the citizens, and a structural reorganization of the service. The new legislation provides for the a priori definition of the universal minimum levels of assistance; these standards are set according to mainly economic factors. Furthermore, the laws in question appear to move definitely away from the principle of free healthcare by passing on a part of the costs to the citizens who make use of the services. Different forms of assistance were also introduced, partially financed by the central government. While re-examining this area of the healthcare service, the setting up of complementary private health funds was significant; these were put in place alongside private pension schemes and show the increasing tendency to allow

43. Act No. 438 of 1992; Law Decree No. 502 of 1992; Act No. 724 of 1994.

private subjects to enter into the health field as well.[44] Reform of the healthcare service also touched on organization of the service itself. Local health units and hospitals became independent: as far as management is involved, they were turned into private companies, and the employment relationships with their workers were also brought under the private-sector rules.

60. In the late 1990s and the early part of the new century, a second wave of reforms, which includes a Constitutional Act geared to increase the local authorities' competencies, has been, on the contrary, an attempt at decentralizing healthcare from a management and finance point of view.[45] Along with the administrative de-centralization currently underway in Italy, the role and independence of the regions in the national healthcare system have been strengthened; they have been given the generality of functions on the matter, but they also now have the financial responsibility for the management of the system. Indeed, under the new laws, the NHS is defined as the set of regional and nationwide healthcare service activities and functions.

61. The NHS, therefore, is a complex organization that involves central government, the regions and communes. Article 1 of Act No. 833 of 1978 defines it as 'that set of functions, structures, services, and activities targeted to the promotion, maintenance, and recovery of the physical and mental health of all the population, with no distinction made as to individual or social differences, and with methods which ensure the equality of all citizens before the service'. In the NHS, the following basic principles are applied:

- principle of totality: cover is not merely provided for the care of the sick, but also for prevention and rehabilitation;
- principle of universal protection;
- principle of equality of treatment;
- principle of planning: the government must prepare a three-year health plan, which must be approved by Parliament; this plan must lay out the general objectives of the NHS;
- principle of democratic participation of the users in the service: participation here means control on the functionality of the healthcare service structures.[46]

§2. Field of Application

62. Following on from the principles of universal and equal care, the subjective scope of the NHS includes all the citizens. Foreigners residing in Italy may apply for health protection from the service. Foreigners who only occasionally reside in

44. Article 10, Law Decree No. 517 of 1993.
45. Act No. 419 of 1998; Law Decree No. 112 and No. 124 of 1998; Law Decree No. 229 of 1999; Law Decree No. 49, No. 56, No. 168, and No. 254 of 2000; Act No. 388 of 2000; Constitutional Act No. 3 of 2001.
46. Law Decree No. 502 of 1992.

Italy are also covered, according, however, to special conditions. Claimants are listed at the local health units where they reside and these lists are periodically updated. They may use the services of the area where they reside; for grounded reasons, or in an emergency, or if they are temporarily living elsewhere, they can also use the services of another area. In relation to claimants, it must be pointed out that, after the 1990s' reforms, only basic services are granted to all citizens. Differentiated types of assistance are only available upon payment of medical fees.

§3. Care Provided

63. The healthcare service provides the following:

- diagnosis and medical care for diseases;
- health training;
- disease and accident prevention (vaccinations, singling out risk factors, workplace health checks, etc.);
- rehabilitation of physical, mental, or sensory disability;
- alimentary health;
- control of the production, sale and distribution of drugs and medicines;
- professional and vocational training of the health operators;
- workplace safety;
- family health;
- school and sports medicine;
- care for the handicapped;
- care for the elderly;
- psychiatric care;
- supply of prosthetics;
- therapeutic o rehabilitative thermal cures;
- forensic medicine;
- rebalancing the social and health conditions in the territory and coordination with environmental policies.

64. The guaranteed care is therefore global in nature. However, after the reforms of the 1990s, the service global nature was partially impaired by the political decision to guarantee only the basic and essential services to everyone; moreover, the actual level of these services depends on available resources. Healthcare service, in particular, takes the following forms:

- General medical cover and paediatric cover: this is provided by General Practitioners (GP), whom the patient chooses from a list of healthcare service doctors or doctors who have a convention with it.
- Specialist care, provided at the ambulatory of the local health units or in clinics that have undersigned a convention with the NHS, upon referral by a GP.
- Nursing care, provided in clinics, hospitals, or at home.
- Hospital assistance, provided by public hospitals or private ones that have undersigned a convention with the NHS.

– Drug care, provided by the supply of medicines on presentation of a GP's prescription.

Healthcare is bound up with the dignity and freedom of the individual patient, which is shown by the patient's right to decide whom to have as a doctor and where to go for treatment. Italian citizens resident in Italy, when so authorized by their local health units, may go abroad for specialist care and are entitled, under certain conditions, to partial reimbursement of their expenses.

65. With the re-shaping of universally guaranteed services, recent legislation has also introduced the following types of differentiated assistance:

– incentives to the use of indirect assistance provided by authorized private clinics by helping patients with expenses for using private medicine;
– the setting up of supplementary health funds, which negotiate, on behalf of their associates, with public or private clinics (which have signed a convention with the NHS), optimal services from a cost-quality point of view; taking part in these schemes means the patient must give up the right to ordinary healthcare. These schemes, which must meet certain basic structural, instrumental, and qualifications requirements, enjoy public financial aids.

66. The most recent reforms have improved quality control in the services provided by the NHS. In particular, the regions and the Health Ministry must make periodic checks on the quality of the services provided. These checks apply efficiency and quality indicators. The communes and patients themselves are asked to monitor service quality and to complain about any faults they notice. Citizens can report these inefficiencies through observations, oppositions, accusations, or administrative complaints to the local health unit's or the hospital's director; these claims can be made personally or through the relevant organizations.

§4. Administrative Structure

67. The organizational structure of the NHS, as set up in 1978, was significantly reformed during the 1990s. The central government runs nationwide health planning. The Health Ministry is entrusted with the general functions of planning, coordinating, and controlling the system, as well as with those laid down by law concerning the healthcare service. The Government, when preparing the three-year health plan, must define uniform levels of assistance (LEA) guaranteed for all citizens. Most operative tasks have been passed over to the regions. The regions, in fact, are in charge of local healthcare. They draw up regional health plans after the national health plan and specify which of the organizing principles are to be used in healthcare services. They also decide how the economic and patrimonial resources, financing, supervision, and control shall be run in local health units and hospitals. They can provide for better levels of health care than those laid down by the government's three-year health plan, under their financial responsibility. They also are entrusted with controls on structural, technological, and organizational requirements, and on the quality of the service offered. The increase of the regional prerogatives in the healthcare system, as we shall see, has been flanked by a considerable increase in the financial responsibilities.

68. The healthcare service reform has also touched on the relationship between the communes and the local health units, and on the juridical-administrative structure of the local health units and hospitals.

In the system outlined in the 1978 law, the town councils already had a very important role in healthcare service management. They fulfilled all the administrative functions not expressly covered by the regions and central government. These functions were to be exercised through the local health unities (ASL or AUSL), which were therefore not independent bodies but merely operative structures of the communes. The health units were therefore a set of functions, services, and offices in local government which – in a particular geographical area – looked after healthcare. Hospitals, on the other hand, were structures of the ASL managed by the town councils.

The 1990s' reforms have changed the ASL into trusts and cut their numbers drastically; their territorial ambit of operation corresponds now to areas defined by the regions. Therefore, the ASL are now agencies of the regions. They are public corporations and have entrepreneurial independence; they are run according to a private contract, and their employment relationships are regulated according to the legislation of the private sector. Within their area, the local health units provide LEA as defined in the nationwide health plans and eventually amended by the regional plans. Together with the region and hospitals, the local health units also supervise and control the correct and efficient use of resources; and finally, they are in charge of supervising the application of workplace health and safety regulations. Hospitals too have been reformed. Hospital trusts have the same structures as the local health trusts; the financing criteria according to which hospitals are run are laid down by the regions. Their budget must be in balance; if there are unjustifiable losses or the impairment of the structural characteristic of the services, the Regional Executive Committee sends a Commissar and the trust loses its independence.

§5. FINANCING

69. Act No. 833 of 1978 stated that the NHS financing was to be provided for by the National Health Fund, which was financed annually by the central government and shared among the regions according to certain pre-set parameters. A further source of financing is the Regional Tax on Productive Activities. Following the Constitutional reform of 2001, however, regions have been given budgeting autonomy and become responsible for supporting the financing of the Health Service. Although the state may intervene to finance underdeveloped territories, the constitution of a state fund to equalize resources for those regions with lower per capita fiscal capacity is also provided. Finally, the service is funded by the so-called tickets, which are a contribution towards healthcare paid by patients when being treated.

70. From the finance point of view, regions must use their own resources to face up to any shortfalls in local health units' and hospital spending and to any payments for the supply of healthcare levels superior to the minimum standards provided in the nationwide plan. In order to meet their obligations, the regions may: raise the amount paid for 'tickets' on medicines, prescriptions, or on prescriptions concerning medical care (provided that lifesaving drugs remain exonerated); lower the maximum levels of expenses for those exonerated from paying the ticket; raise regional taxes and contributions.

71. As stated above, healthcare services require patients to contribute towards health costs.

At the moment, however, the following are free to patients:

- instrumental and laboratory diagnosis and other specialist care included in early warning and collective prevention programmes realized under regional or nationwide health plans or under projects authorized at the regional or provincial level;
- diagnostic and instrumental tests for detecting tumours in the female genital tract, breast cancer, rectal cancers;
- diagnostic and instrumental tests for detecting neoplasia in the young and in high-risk people below the age of 45, according to the criteria defined by ministerial decree;
- diagnostic and laboratory tests and other techniques for specialist healthcare in compulsory collective schemes or ordered at local level during epidemics or finalized at starting work;
- general medical and paediatric care;
- care during maternity;
- services relative to the prevention of the spread of the human HIV virus;
- services provided to promote the donation of blood, organs, or tissues;
- services provided to care for patients with irreversible complications as a result of compulsory vaccinations, or the transfusion or administration of blood products;
- compulsory and advised vaccinations for children;
- treatments provided while the patient is in hospital.

Other forms of drug care, specialist clinic visits, instrumental and laboratory diagnoses and thermal cures are conditioned to the payment of a ticket. In particular, the patient is required to pay a fixed proportion for each prescription or particular cure; patients may also be asked by regions to pay part of the drugs bought, except for lifesaving ones. Furthermore, patients must pay for specialist cures and instrumental and laboratory diagnoses, up to a maximum fixed by law. Any region states then the exemptions from tickets for particular categories of patients. The following are generally exempted from ticket payment, provided that their income does not exceed certain fixed limits: young (under 6 years of age) patients and over sixty-seven pensioners; civil, war, service, and work invalids, pensioners and the unemployed; patients with specific disease types such as oncologic, chronic, invalidating, or rare.

§6. SUPPLEMENTARY HEALTH FUNDS

72. The legislator has also regulated the institution of supplementary health funds.[47] These funds provide services that are additional to those of the State Health Service; they also provide for payment of the patients' tickets owed for services granted by the NHS. The services are direct: to both public and private employees; to the self-employed; to freelance professionals; and to individuals, however they subscribe in the forms of cover set out by law, which is to say, in a self-managed form or entrusted by agreement with a mutual aid society or with authorized insurance companies. The institution documents of these funds may be: contracts or collective agreements, which may be for companies; agreements between the self-employed or between freelance professionals, promoted by the respective associations; the regulations of boards or companies or local authorities or non-profit associations or mutual aid societies that are legally recognized.

47. Article 9, Law Decree No. 502/1992.

Chapter 2. Sickness Benefits for Common Diseases

§1. Field of Application

I. The Concept of Disease

73. In social insurance terms, disease is considered to be any alteration in the state of health that lasts more than three days and requires the assistance of a doctor or surgeon or the administration of therapy. Italian constitutional case law[48] has defined disease as not merely an acute pathological situation causing current inability to work, but as including every malaise which, although it does not exclude the patient from work, requires therapies incompatible with working activity and which cannot be put off until the patient goes on holiday.

74. There have been long discussions about how to bring thermal cures back into the system. The diseases that can be cured in this way are listed by way of a decree from the Health Ministry. Only those thermal cures that treat the listed diseases can be publicly financed. Therapy can be undertaken outside annual holiday periods or ordinary leave, provided that a prescription for them is signed by a healthcare service specialist where it is required a prompt treatment; treatment must take place within thirty days of the doctor's request.

II. The Subjective Scope of Protection

75. Patients who are covered by sickness benefits include the following:

- workers in industry and assimilated categories;
- agricultural labourers;
- home workers;
- traders and similar workers;
- the collaborators continuous and coordinated and the self-employed enrolled in the INPS scheme reserved for them.

The following are not covered: white-collar workers; workers in domestic or family service; building guardians; doorkeepers; travelling salesmen; political party and trades union employees. In these cases, the employer takes care of cover for his/her staff.

§2. Amount of Benefits

76. Daily sickness benefit is paid from the fourth day onwards, for a maximum of 180 days per annum. The amount paid varies according to the work category the

48. Constitutional Court, 18 Dec. 1987, No. 559.

patient belongs to, but is usually 50% of the usual wage and rises to two-thirds when the illness is prolonged. The waiting days period is not operative in case relapse or new illness intervened within thirty days. With temporary jobs, benefits are paid for a period that cannot be superior to the number of days worked in the previous twelve months. Sickness pay may be paid also for diseases arisen up to sixty days after the worker has left his/her job. Sickness pay is usually paid in advance by the employer, and it is then counted as an advance on national insurance contributions owed by the employer to INPS, upon which lays the final burden. Eligibility is limited to one year after the day the illness became apparent. The worker on sick leave is entitled to notional contributions up to a maximum of twenty-four months, but after twelve months, notional contributions are worth only 50% in pension calculations. It must be added here that almost all collective bargaining agreements require the employer both to make up the daily sickness allowance to the sick worker's normal wage and to pay the waiting days.

77. The right to sickness pay depends on certification of the worker, who must also undergo medical controls. Workers who fail to send the medical certification to INPS within two days lose their entitlement to pay for one day per day's delay, unless he/she can show a valid reason for the delay.[49] A worker who is not at home when medical controls are carried out loses entitlement for ten days; if the worker is not at home when the next medical control is made, he/she loses entitlement to 50% of total sickness pay from the eleventh day to the end of sick leave.[50]

§3. Conditions

78. The general nature of the NHS has not meant that the partial and differentiated forms of sickness pay benefits, which already existed beforehand, were equalled out. Indeed, workers and employers still have to pay the same differentiated contributions that were paid to the former welfare agencies. The various sickness pay benefits are now all managed by INPS. Contributions towards sickness pay coverage are calculated as a percentage of the taxable earning of the beneficiary. Contribution is usually about 2.5%, but ministerial decrees may increase it. Contributions are also owed by employers who, whether through law or agreement with the workers, pay their own sickness pay allowance.[51]

49. *See* on this issue Constitutional Court, 29 Dec. 1988, No. 1143.
50. *See* Constitutional Court, 26 Jan. 1988, No. 78.
51. Cassazione S.U. 27.6.2003, No. 10232.

Chapter 3. Compulsory Tuberculosis Insurance

§1. Field of Application

79. Everyone who has reached the age of 14 and who is in paid employment is entitled to Compulsory Tuberculosis Insurance, except civil servants and local government employees, unless they are working in the public health sector. The following are covered: agricultural workers; those who work at home; primary school teachers and headmasters; light maritime and lake fishermen. Family members of the above are also covered. Finally, as a consequence of Act No. 88 of 1987, coverage is provided for all citizens who earn less than the legal minimum for income tax purposes, even when they are not obliged to pay the contributions or have not been working long enough.

§2. Amount of Benefits

80. Act No. 88 of 1987 has reshaped the discipline of benefits paid to tuberculosis victims. They are entitled to:

- a daily allowance for hospitalization, paid as long as the patient is in a hospital or on clinical cure; this is of the same amount of the sick pay, for one-hundred and eighty days; then its amount is equal to the social allowance;
- a post-sanatorium indemnity for two years after the daily allowance stops if recovery is made or the disease stabilizes, provided the patient spent at least two months in hospital or on clinical cures; its amount is the same of the social allowance;
- a daily allowance for clinical cures, when the cure lasts at least two months and is followed by a stabilization;
- a monthly allowance for cure and maintenance for two years (renewable), paid after the post-sanatorium indemnity expires, provided it can be shown that the patient has lost at least half his/her earning capacity in suitable jobs as a result of tuberculosis.

When the beneficiary is a member of the insured worker's family or is in receipt of an INPS pension or of an INAIL annuity, the amounts are halved. On the other hand, benefits are increased for family members maintained by the claimant; the supplement is of the same amount as family income support. A Christmas bonus, increased for family members maintained by the claimant, and the notional contribution are also paid to the claimant under this scheme.

§3. CONDITIONS

81. Economic benefits for tuberculosis victims, set up in 1927, are paid for by compulsory tuberculosis insurance managed by INPS.[52] The relative healthcare is the responsibility of the NHS. Given that the gravity of this disease has been greatly reduced, the premiums are now paid by the central government.

82. Coverage is given, provided that the tuberculosis patient is admitted to hospital or uses special environmental or home therapies. Another condition is that at least one year's worth of insurance and contributions must have been paid in; the onset of the disease is unimportant in relation to the setting up of the insurance relationship. In other words, coverage is provided even if the disease began before the setting up of the insurance relationship.

52. Act No. 419 of 1975; Act No. 88 of 1987; Act No. 488 of 1998.

Part IV. Family Allowances

Chapter 1. Social Insurance and Assistance for Families

83. In this part of the study, we shall look at all forms of social insurance and assistance for families. The need for social care for families is recognized by the Italian Constitution, and more specifically in Articles 29, 30, 31, and 37. In particular, the Republic undertakes the duty to provide maintenance for children when their parents are unable to do it; another duty of the state is that of promoting, through economic measures and other benefits, the formation of families and the fulfilment of the relative duties, especially as regards large families. The idea of the family used in the welfare system varies; the exact definition depends on specific requirements and political choices, which may change as the circumstances demand. It is worth mentioning Act No. 76/2016 here, which states that whenever in legislation the words 'spouse' and 'marriage' are used, these must be intended as including the civil union between persons of the same sex and the two parties of the union.

The welfare provisions for families are the following:

- leave for assistance to family members;
- rest and leave of absence;
- general family allowance;
- pensions and accident provisions for unpaid care workers;
- social assistance benefits for low-income families.

Time off from work, rests, leave of absence, and maternity benefits, covered by Act No. 1204 of 1974 and Act No. 903 of 1977, consolidated and amended by Act No. 53 of 2000, were re-ordered and coordinated under the Legislative Decree No. 151 of 2001 on the protection of maternity and paternity.[53]

84. Among the means used to assist the family, notional contributions are often utilized.[54] In addition to the instances we shall see when dealing with time off from work, rests and leaves of absence,[55] the pension reform of 1995 introduced (for those paying in contributions to the new system) up to 160 days per child of notional national insurance contributions for parents who take time off from work to educate or assist children up to the age of 6. Furthermore, twenty-five days per annum of

53. *See also* Ministerial Decree No. 278 of 21 Jul. 2000.
54. Act No. 335 of 1995.
55. *See* Ch. 2 below.

notional contributions, within the period of twenty-four months, are calculated for parents who take time off work to assist children above 6 years of age, or their spouse, or a live-in parent, provided that there are situations of handicap. Another method used by legislation is bringing the retirement age forward: working mothers may retire four months early for each child, up to a maximum of twelve months. As an alternative to that, the pension age of the working mother can be virtually increased by one year when she has one or two children, or by two years when she has three children or more. Finally, more favourable coefficients of transformation are fixed for maternity, in relation to which the increment of one year of the coefficient of transformation for one or two children and two years for three or more is laid down; coefficients of transformation are the multiplier of the individual contribution total and are linked to life expectancy and age of retirement.[56]

56. *See* on this Part VIII of this study.

Chapter 2. Leaves and Time Off from Work to Assist Family Members

§1. Maternity and Paternity Leave

I. Maternity Leave

85. Italian law lays down a period of compulsory absence for working mothers, during which any working activity is absolutely forbidden. Non-compliance with this law is punishable with up to six months' arrest. This period usually goes from two months before the presumed date of childbirth, until three months afterwards. The period includes:

– the time between the presumed and effective dates of childbirth, when this is later than the presumed date;
– the days not used up before childbirth if the baby is born before the presumed date of delivery; these days are added to the period of maternity leave after the birth.

The ban on making a pregnant woman work is brought forward to three months before the presumed date of the birth when she works in a job considered to be too dangerous or hard in relation to the advanced state of pregnancy. These particular types of jobs are determined in decrees issued by the Employment Ministry, which considers recommendations made by the most representative trade unions. A further bringing forward of the period of maternity leave may be necessary when there are grave complications in the pregnancy, or when the woman cannot be moved to another position where she or her baby's health is not jeopardized. This provision is applied by inspectors from the Employment Ministry, on the basis of a medical exam carried out by the relevant organs of the NHS.

Act No. 53 of 2000 allowed a more flexible period for maternity leave, postponing the beginning of it to a month before the presumed birth, and continuing it until four months after childbirth. The use of this facility cannot change the total leave period allowed. This flexible leave depends, however, on a certificate issued by both a doctor from the NHS and the doctor in charge of health and safety at work in the relevant workplace, stating that this will not harm the woman or the unborn child. The flexible period is also excluded for certain types of jobs as specified in ministerial decrees.

Alternatively, women can take the five months maternity leave entirely after the birth, provided that an NHS specialist deems that there is no risk to the mother and to the unborn child (Article 1, paragraph 485 of Act No. 145/2018, which has amended Article 16 of Decree No. 151/2001). Although this measure is likely to be appreciated by working mothers and has been prudently accompanied by a thorough medical evaluation, it also raised some critics as regards the risk of exposing women, most of all precarious workers, to possible pressures to keep on working until the birth of the child.

Maternity leave is also granted in the case of national and international adoption or fostering. In case of adoption, the leave must be taken during the first five months after the child comes to live in the family and it lasts five months (with no limits as to the age of the child). In case of fostering, the leave has to be taken during the first five months after the child comes in the family and it lasts three months. In case of international adoption or fostering, maternity leave can be taken also during the period of permanence in the territory of the country involved in the adoption or fostering; alternatively time off is granted.

As well as for natural mothers, these periods can be postponed once only if the child is in hospital.

Abortion, finally, is considered to all extents and purposes to be the same as birth, if it occurs more than 180 days after conception; otherwise, it is treated as sickness.

86. During the whole period of maternity leave, mothers are entitled to a daily indemnity paid by INPS. The same is paid to fathers who take advantage of paternity leave. Italian law guarantees the right to this benefit to the following categories: private and public employees, in all productive areas, including managers, part-time workers, home workers, or domestic workers; self-employed; professionals, although in this case entitlement to benefit does not require the suspension or interruption of work; coordinated and continuative collaborators of the employer; public utility workers.

87. Maternity benefits do not require a minimum amount of national insurance contributions to have been paid in: it is enough that the claimant was regularly employed at the time the compulsory leave period began. This is also the case when the worker has been made redundant; the benefit is also paid when the firm ceases its activity or the employment contract expires during the period of compulsory leave. Benefit is again paid to pregnant women who, at the beginning of the leave, have been suspended, are absent without pay from work, or are unemployed, provided that no more than sixty days have passed between the beginning of the leave and that of the suspension, absence, or unemployment. If a woman has been unemployed for no more than sixty days since the period of leave, she may apply for maternity benefit instead of unemployment benefit; if she is not entitled to unemployment benefit, she may still apply for maternity benefit, provided that no more than one-hundred and eighty days have passed between the beginning of the leave and that of the unemployment, and that during the last two years the woman has paid in at least twenty-six weeks' worth of maternity contributions. Finally, pregnant women whose maternity leave started sixty days after the beginning of a suspension from work, and who are in receipt of short-time earning funds, are entitled to maternity benefit instead of the latter. The laws governing such complex interactions between the different benefits were passed because often maternity benefit is higher than the various unemployment allowances. For women in the private sector, the amount of maternity indemnity is 80% of their average overall daily wage. The wage used to make this calculation is that earned over the month or four weeks before the period of compulsory leave. In other cases, that is, for temporary agricultural labourers for the self-employed, the benefit is calculated according to a conventionally set daily wage. For self-employed professional women, though, calculations are based on a percentage of their declared earnings over the second year before maternity, but the benefit cannot be less than a certain ceiling granted by law. Women in the civil service, according to their employment contract, are entitled to an amount equal to their full wage. The benefit is paid in advance by the employer, who is then reimbursed by the INPS through a corresponding reduction of the owed ordinary social insurance contributions. INPS pays the benefit directly to: agricultural workers and temporary agricultural labourers; women who work in domestic services; the unemployed women and those suspended from work who are not in receipt of short-time earning funds. To all effects and purposes, periods of maternity leave count towards the length of service: indeed, maternity leave is to be counted as actual work as regards seniority, annual vacations, thirteenth-month salary payments, for the purposes of promotion and for that of wage incentives; periods of maternity leave are to be regarded as periods of employment, unless special requirements have been made for that purpose by collective agreements. Moreover, when a woman is on maternity leave, notional contributions are counted towards her pension right and amount. If she is no longer employed, however, these notional contributions are only counted if she has already paid in at least five years' worth of national insurance contributions. Entitlement to benefit expires one year after it was granted. Another provision, Article 1 paragraph 239 of Act No. 234/2021 addressed, recently, autonomous workers with low revenues: in case their annual income in the year before the birth of the child is lower than EUR 8,145,00 indexed to inflation, they can benefit by three additional months of maternity allowance.

88. At the end of the compulsory period of absence, women are entitled to return to work in the same productive unit as before or in another productive unit of the same firm located in the same commune, unless they expressly renounce this right. They cannot be discharged until the child is 1 year old. They have a right to carry out the same job as before or an equivalent one. Furthermore, Act No. 101/2008 lays down the right of a woman on maternity leave to benefit at the end of this period from any improvement in working conditions to which she would have been entitled during her absence.

II. Paternity Leave

89. Paternity leave is granted to the father after the birth for the whole length of the maternity leave or for the remaining period in special cases, like: the mother, including a professional and self-employed mother, dies or becomes seriously ill; in the event of the abandonment of the child; if the child is in the exclusive custody of the father. Adoptive and foster fathers can also take the paternity leave in place of the maternity leave of the mothers in the same special cases (Article 31 of Decree No. 151/2001). The same economic and working conditions as well as notional contributions provided for the maternity leave are granted to the father.

Furthermore, according to Article 4, paragraph 24, of Act No. 92/2012,[57] fathers are also entitled to ten days paid compulsory paternity leave in the first five months

57. As modified by Art. 1, para. 205, Act No. 208 of 28 Dec. 2015, by Art. 1, para. 354, Act No. 232/2016, by Art. 1 para. 278, Act No. 145/2018, by art. 1 para. 363 and 364, Act No. 178/2020 and by art. 1 para. 134, Act No. 234/2021, which finally made these measures permanent.

following the child's birth. The latter can also be used at the same time as the mother's compulsory leave and is added to the paternity leave. Moreover, fathers are entitled to one day paid optional leave, alternatively to the mother, within the first five months following the child's birth. These forms of leave are also granted in the case of national and international adoption or fostering. Periods of paid leave are taken into account for pension purposes.

§2. Parental Leave

90. Parental leave is optional and lasts a total of ten months; it may be taken by either the father or the mother during the first twelve years of the child's life, or during the twelve years since the child entered the family in the case of adoption or fostering, independently of age (however, the leave cannot be taken when the child comes of age). In particular, the following have this right: the mother, when the period of compulsory maternity leave ends, for a total of six months at a time, all at once or broken into smaller fractions; the father, when his child is born, for a continuous or split period of no more than six months, which may be extended to seven when the father decides to take the leave for a continuous or split period of no less than three months; single parents, for a continuous or split period of not more than ten months.

If a working father decides to take no less than three months off from work, the total time allowed to both parents is eleven months. This law is evidently an incentive for working fathers to take leave.

Parents of severely handicapped children may take up to three years off from work in parental leave, provided the child is not hospitalized in a specialized institute. This extension of parental leave is an alternative to legally sanctioned rests and special leave for parents of handicapped children. The extension begins with the end of the maximum period of parental leave.

Parental leave can be taken for one continuous period or various periods. The means of application of the parental leave on an hourly basis are stipulated by collective agreements or by the law (Article 32 of Decree No. 151/2001).

91. During the periods of parental leave, for the first six years of the child's life (or during the first six years from the day that the child enters the family in the case of adoption or official custody),[58] parents are entitled to a benefit equal to 30% of their normal wages for a total of six months for both parents. So out of the ten (or eleven) months only six are paid. Notional contributions are taken into account for pension rights and amounts. This also applies to the period of an extension of the leave for parents of severely handicapped children. For any leave taken after the child reaches the age of 6, or over the maximum period of six months, the benefit is only paid if the claimant's earnings are less than 2.5 times the minimum pension paid under the general compulsory insurance system and for children aged not over 8. In this case, the notional contribution calculations for pension purposes are

58. Article 9 of Decree No. 80/2015, which amended Decree No. 151/2001, extended this period to six years.

reduced, but the amount can be fully supplemented through redemption of contributions (Articles 34 and 35 of Decree No. 151/2001).

§3. Leave for Illness of a Child

92. Both parents, alternatively, may take time off from work if a child less than 3 years of age becomes ill; the leave is allowed to last for the whole duration of the child's illness. The parents, alternatively, may also take up to five days per annum off from work, if a child between 3 and 8 years of age becomes ill. For entitlement to this leave, the parent must present a certificate issued by a specialist doctor of the NHS. Leave of absence for a sick child is unpaid. However, notional contributions are calculated when the child is younger than three. These are reduced when the child is between 3 and 8, but the amount can be fully made up through the redemption of contributions. Periods of leave of absence for a sick child count towards a worker's length of service, but they do not count as regards paid or unpaid holidays and Christmas bonuses. Leave is also allowed, with higher age limits, when the child has been adopted or a parent has official custody. The same regulations apply to the civil service. Civil servants, however, enjoy more favourable collective bargaining conditions than workers in the private sector (Articles 47–52 Decree No. 151/2001).

§4. Leave for Relatives and Spouse of Seriously Handicapped Persons

93. Article 42, paragraph 5 of Decree No. 151/2001 states that workers in the private or public sector who take care of a severely disabled cohabiting spouse who is not hospitalized (unless continuous assistance is required in hospital) may take a continuous or split period of up to two years off from work. If there is no cohabiting spouse, then this right belongs to the parents of the disabled person. This two-year period may be used only once in an entire working life. The benefit during this period is the same as the last salary earned, up to a maximum of EUR 43,579 per year; this figure is constantly reviewed; the period of leave is covered by notional contributions, but it does not accrue the length of service. The leave is paid by the employer, who then deducts the amount from what is owed to the relative welfare agency.

94. Article 33 of Act No. 104/1992 states that workers in the private or public sector who take care of a severely disabled relative who is not hospitalized are granted three consecutive days of leave a month. Both parents, including adoptive parents, of a severely disabled child are entitled to this leave and can use it alternately. The leave also applies to the guardian of a severely disabled person. For these periods of leave, a benefit equal to the claimant's normal wage is paid. The period of leave is covered by figurative/notional contributions. Article 33 also provides (in paragraph 2) that working parents, also adoptive, of a seriously handicapped child of less than 3 years of age are entitled to two hours' paid rest per day; for these periods of rest a benefit equal to the claimant's normal wage is paid. A reduced form of notional contribution calculations is applied to this benefit, but a redemption of contributions can be made to fill the gap that is left.

§5. Leave for Special Events and Causes

95. This type of leave covers: death or serious illness; serious family reasons.

The first type of leave may be taken by a private or public sector employee upon the death or serious illness of a spouse (even if he/she is legally separated), or of another relative within the second degree, whether or not they lived together, or of anybody who belongs to the certified family of the employee. Leave consists in the right to take a maximum of three days per year off from work. The wage for the days of leave is paid by the employer, so this is not a publicly financed welfare. Instead of taking time off from work for documented cases of a relative's serious illness, the worker may contract some different working arrangement with the employer.

Leave for serious family reasons is granted for a maximum of two years, during which time the employer must keep the worker's post; this leave is, however, unpaid. Workers who take time off from work for this reason may not do any other work. Leave may be taken all at once or in fractions. The two-year period may be used only once in an entire working life. A request may be made by the worker, whether in the private or public sector, for personal reasons, for reasons concerning a member of the certified family or one of the subjects obliged to pay the aliments pursuant to Article 433 of the Civil Procedure Code (spouse, natural or adopted children, close relatives, adoptive or natural parents, son-in-law and daughter-in-law, father-in-law and mother-in-law, brothers and sisters). Serious family reasons are to be understood as: necessity caused by the death of one of the above-named relatives, care and assistance for the same, situations of serious personal discomfort (not including disease), particular diseases (as defined in a ministerial decree) among relatives, or the death of a relative for which there is no other form of leave. The employer may deny the worker leave of absence, provided an adequate explanation is given.

Leave of absence or unpaid leave does not add to the length of service, whereas voluntary payments or redemption may be made to fill the gap in pension contributions (Article 4 of Act No. 53/2000).

The leave for serious family reasons has been extended also to parents, relatives, and relatives-in-law within the third degree of the disabled, even if they do not live together. The maximum period of leave is two years, and is applicable even when the disabled person is in a special institute. Those who take leave for serious family reasons are not entitled to pay, but can make up the gap in their pension contributions by redemption or voluntary payments. They are entitled to return to their old jobs when the period ends. The leave has to be authorized by the employer, who may deny it, provided an adequate explanation linked to organizational or productive reasons is given.[59]

59. *See*, on the leave for special events or causes, the Ministerial Decree No. 278 of 21 Jul. 2000.

§6. Maternity Benefit for Atypical and Discontinuous Workers

96. Benefit is paid for each child born, or for every child adopted or fostered from 2 July 2000 onwards. With adopted or fostered children under six, the benefit is paid from the time they enter the new family; there are no age limits for adoption from foreign countries. Benefit is granted to Italian citizens resident in Italy, and EU citizens resident in Italy or holding a valid residence permit, for whom contributions have been paid in the maternity social insurance scheme. The benefit is index-linked. It is paid fully if the mother is not entitled to any social insurance maternity leave benefit, whereas the maternity benefit is paid for an amount equal to the difference between the two benefits when the woman is in receipt of a social insurance maternity benefit, the amount of which is inferior to that of the maternity benefit described above. The benefit is paid by INPS. Instead of paying it to the mother, it can be paid to others, and in particular to the father, provided that the right conditions set by a specific ministerial decree are in place.

§7. Basic Maternity Allowance

97. Mothers without any other maternity benefits are granted a maternity allowance for children born after 1 January 2001 or adopted or fostered from that day. The benefit is paid to Italian or EU citizens who are resident in Italy or holders of an Italian residence permit; the benefit is index-linked; however, to qualify for this benefit, the family income must be below a certain level.

The basic maternity allowance is provided by the Town Council but is paid out by INPS. Fathers can be eligible for the same benefit, as an alternative to the mother, in the cases set out in the relative ministerial decrees.

§8. Daily Rest for Mothers and Fathers

98. Employers must allow working mothers, during the first year of the child's life, to take two rest periods of one hour each, which may be added and taken during the working day. In the case of multiple births, the rest periods are doubled. Rest periods are considered to be working hours for the sake of work and pay. A reduced figurative/notional contribution is recognized during the rest periods, but the gap can be made up through a redemption of contributions. These regulations also apply in the case of adopted or foster children for the first year of the child's life within the family. Rest periods are granted to fathers in the following cases: when children are under the father's exclusive custody; as an alternative to the working mother; when the mother is not employed; when the mother dies or becomes seriously ill. In the event of multiple births, the father may decide to use the extra time allowed (Articles 39–41 of Decree No. 151/2001).

§9. Bonus Kindergarten

99. According to Article 1, paragraph 355, Act No. 232/2016 (as modified by Article 1 paragraph 343, Act No. 160/2019) children born/adopted on or after 1 January 2016 are entitled to an annual contribution of up to EUR 3,000.00, for the payment of fees for attending authorized public and private nurseries and for forms of home assistance in favour of children under the age of 3 suffering from serious chronic diseases. The benefit is paid to Italian or EU citizens, who are resident in Italy and to non-EU citizens who are resident in Italy and holders of an EU or Italian residence permit; however, to qualify for this benefit, the ISEE of the children must be below a certain level.[60] The benefit amount also depends on the ISEE of the children. The benefit is paid by INPS. The bonus required, both for nursery schools and for forms of support at home, can be paid, within the specified spending limit (for 2022, it is EUR 553.8 million), according to the order in which the online application is submitted. Any applications that, based on the timing of presentation, due to insufficient budget, cannot be accepted will in any case be taken into consideration: if at the end of the year sums are still available, the same applications can be recovered and processed according to the order of presentation acquired.

60. ISEE is a value which includes all movable, immovable properties and annual income of the household. ISEE is self-certified by the applicant through a calculation system made available by INPS.

Chapter 3. General Family Allowance

§1. Field of Application

100. Family benefits in Italy have always been characterized by a double function: raising low earnings to an acceptable level and meeting the needs linked to the maintenance of a family. These benefits are justified by Article 36 of the Italian Constitution, which guarantees sufficient earnings for the worker and his/her family, and Article 31, which requires the central government to take initiatives in favour of the family. These allowances also apply to civil unions between persons of the same sex (Act No. 76/2016). A reform law passed in 1988 introduced the Family Income Support, which unified the different benefits for private-and public-sector workers.[61] Recently, however, this area of legislation underwent a deep reform. In particular, Act. No. 46 of 1 April 2021 delegated the Government to reorganize, simplify and strengthen different forms of economic support for families providing for a unique and general allowance to be recognized for each dependent child. Decrees should have been issued, before 21 April 2022, to implement Act No. 46, which is aimed at promoting the birth rate, financially supporting parents, and promoting employment, especially for women. The new family allowance should respect the principles of universality and gradualness and be intended to replace many of the previous family benefits. Act No. 46/2021 was finally implemented by Decree No. 230/2021. Following the principles stated by Delegation Act No 46/2021, the new measure addresses all families, regardless of parental income and work activity and replaces the birth bonus, the birth allowance, the family income support, the family income supplement for low-earning families and the tax deductions for dependent children under the age of 21. Overall, the reform modernizes our welfare system making it simpler, more transparent and inclusive. Child support will increase for most Italian families, especially for parents who were little or not at all protected (such as, self-employed, long-term unemployed and atypical workers). Nevertheless, considering that the new grant substitutes several measures, it is quite hard to value its real impact on some categories. Moreover, the reform will probably weaken the sustainability of families of employees with a low or medium income. In order to avoid this risk a safeguard clause has been provided to guarantee an automatic compensation for the next three years. Households are entitled to the new general family allowance from the seventh month of pregnancy up to the 21st year of age of the dependent child attending school or university or working or working on an internship (on condition that his/her annual income is lower than EUR 8,000) or searching for a job. It is addressed to a wide audience of beneficiaries, including self-employed workers and persons receiving income support. In case of disabled children, the grant is recognized with no age limit.

---

61. Act No. 153 of 1988.

§2. Amount of the Benefits

101. The allowance will be paid by the INPS (National Institute for Social Security) following the submission of an annual application. The amount of this benefit is modulated on the basis of the total economic condition of the household, measured by the ISEE, and the age of the dependent child; it also takes into consideration the possible effect of disincentive to work for the second earner in the household. Households whose ISEE is lower than EUR 15,000.00 are entitled to a grant of EUR 175.00 per child. This amount decreases as the ISEE increases, until it stabilizes at EUR 50.00 per month, per child, for ISEE equal or higher than EUR 40,000.00. This basic sum decreases to a range within a minimum of EUR 25.00 and a maximum of EUR 85.00 in case of adult sons. Different increases are to be added for: each child following the second one, households with more than four children, mothers under the age of 21, households with two income earners and children with disability. In case of disabled children, its amount also depends on the severity of the disability (for children under age).

102. The general family allowance is financed by the State and by contributions exclusively paid by employers.

Chapter 4. Pensions and Industrial Accidents Benefits

§1. The Social Insurance Fund for Unpaid Care Workers

103. Family welfare has recently seen the passing of some laws concerning care workers. One of these deals with the Social Insurance Fund for unpaid care workers (Law Decree No. 565/1996).

This replaces the barely used Housewives' Pension Fund, which used to pay invalidity benefits and old-age pensions to housewives who were not in receipt of other social insurance benefits. The fund covers men and women who carry out unpaid and not dependent work within the family, provided that they are not under a contract of employment or self-employed or entitled to a pension. Part-time workers are covered by the fund, even if they work with continuity, provided that the insurance period matured for the right to pension within the social insurance compulsory scheme is shortened as a consequence of the hours reduction.

The fund is purely voluntary. The system used to manage funds is of the capitalization type.

Monthly contribution to the fund cannot be inferior to a certain amount. If a claimant applies after the age of 60, his/her length-of-service contributions can be increased so as to meet the minimum requirements by paying the outstanding balance. An additional contribution to the fund is required for management costs purposes; the management costs are ascertained by specific accounts, while their congruity is verified every five years. The additional contribution is set down in ministerial decrees.

104. Claimants are entitled to the following services:

- a pension, payable from the age of 57 onwards, provided that at least five years' contributions have been made and that the pension matured is not less than 1.2 times the social allowance;
- a pension, payable from the age of 65, provided that at least five years' contributions have been made;
- an inability pension, provided that the claimant has paid in at least five years' contributions and that he/she is totally and permanently unable to do any type of work.

The amount of the pension is calculated according to the contributive system used for the compulsory pension scheme.

§2. Insurance Against Accidents at Home

105. This insurance is compulsory. It covers 18- to 65-year olds doing exclusively unpaid care work in the family. The claimants of this benefit must not do any other sort of work that requires them to take part in compulsory social insurance schemes. The insurance is against accidents that occur while doing care work in the home and are a result of this. The home is understood to mean a building where the family lives, any relative appurtenances and the space of joint ownership. The only benefit paid under this system is permanent disability allowance, provided that the invalidity is higher than 27%.

Part V. Incapacity to Work

Chapter 1. Field of Application

§1. The Private Employment

106. Invalidity benefits were for a long time one of the main financial burdens on INPS. Indeed, invalidity benefits had the function of social assistance benefits for unemployment. The old regulations, reformed in 1984, were based on the loss of earning capacity in work suitable to that normally carried out by the claimant. In order to ascertain invalidity, the claimant had to undergo not only medical controls, but tests were applied to calculate the socio-economic importance of the particular claim: indeed, the claimant's earning capacity is necessarily linked to the socio-economic situation of the territory where the claimant lives and works. The crucial point is that the socio-economic evolution took into account the claimant's employment prospects, especially in the South of Italy, where unemployment is much higher. This factor, when considered together with the lack of an acceptable cover for the unemployed, often meant that the invalidity pensions were used instead of unemployment benefits in farming and depressed areas. Socio-economic factors often allowed the local INPS offices to use certain social insurance benefits as social assistance benefits, according to the employment and economic characteristics of the area where claimants lived. On the other hand, real controls on loss of earnings – as indeed those on the loss of working capacity – were still an extremely controversial matter. Controls were not merely based on technical measurements, but also took into account concrete situations, and the sensitivity and attitude of the benefits agency involved often came into play.

107. The regulations introduced under Act No. 222 of 12 June 1984, which were preceded by repeated reform attempts, completely reshaped the system. Earning capacity was replaced by working capacity. The Parliament tried for the most part to put an end to social assistance policies generated by invalidity benefits. The law also introduced two new levels of invalidity, and thus brought Italian regulations up to the standards applied under European Community law. In relation to both levels of invalidity, there are two benefits of a different regime and amount.

108. The aim of this part of the Italian social insurance system is to provide coverage for people suffering from long-term diseases that cause work inability. Thus, the law protects, in substance, workers who become permanently – although not necessarily absolutely and definitely – unable to continue to earn a wage. Under this scheme, the inability to work due to common illness is covered. Another type of coverage exists, on the other hand, for those hit by professional risks.[62] Invalidity and disability benefit for employees caused by common risks is provided by a specific fund which is also used to pay pensions in the event of old age or death. The scheme is managed by INPS and is known as the compulsory insurances scheme for old age, invalidity, and survivors.

109. Invalidity benefits are paid by the social insurance system, and, like all insurance schemes, that for invalidity has selective functions. Entitlement to benefits is granted only to those workers who have already entered the labour market and paid a minimum of contributions. Benefit rights, as we shall see, are also conditioned by specific contributions requirements: invalidity benefits, in substance, are only paid when the relative illness is recent in respect to employment.

§2. The Public Employment

110. The civil service, up to the pension reform brought in with Act No. 335 in 1995, enjoyed different invalidity benefit regulations from the private sector. The pension reform brought the different common risk regimes together, and the principles laid down in Act No. 222 of 1984 extended to the civil service, although limited to inability only, that is, to the total and permanent impossibility of working. In the civil service, in fact, the mere reduction in the capacity to work, even if a stable one, that is, invalidity, is covered by sick leave regulations; in this case, the regulations on termination of employment because of inability eventually may come into play. As of 1 January 1996, if work ceases due to non-work-related infirmity, as a result of which the claimant is permanently and totally unable to carry out any gainful employment, the worker is entitled to the inability pension.

62. Part VI of this study.

Chapter 2. Conditions

§1. Working Capacity

111. The loss of ability to work is the main requirement for entitlement to benefits. Indeed, the legislation introduced in 1984 has replaced earning capacity with working capacity as the reference term for invalidity benefits. Distinction is made between invalidity and inability, and benefits for the two situations are different. The term 'invalidity' is applied to workers whose working capacity in suitable occupations has been permanently reduced because of a physical or mental defect to less than a third. 'Inability', on the other hand, is applied to workers who are totally and permanently unable to work, because of permanent physical or mental defects or infirmities. The concept of working capacity remains linked to the worker's subjective situation; this thanks to the reference to the claimant's suitable occupation, that is, to the claimant's attitudinal capacity. The new regulations also lay down that an invalidity pre-existing the social insurance relationship equally entitles a claimant to benefit payments, provided that the disease worsens or other infirmities supervene. The permanence of the claimant's invalidity or inability must be confirmed by a rigorous ascertainment procedure, which is an onus for the claimant. These controls may be ordered at any time by the welfare agency. The claimant who refuses to undergo the medical tests without good reasons loses benefits until he accepts the controls.

As regards the legal disputes on invalidity benefits, Act No. 111/2011 introduced a compulsory preventive assessment procedure on the medical condition of the claimants, which is an admissibility condition for the legal action.

§2. Insurance and Contributions Requirements

112. Invalidity benefits are subject to a minimum of contributions, consisting of three years' contributions during the five years preceding a claim. Claimants must also have been insured for at least five years. Insurance and contributions requirements may also be met while the procedural formalities are being absolved or during the adjudications procedure: they do not necessarily need to be already fulfilled by the time of the claim. Benefits, however, will be paid from the moment when the requirements are met.

Civil service claimants have the same contributions requirements as workers in the private sector.

Chapter 3. Benefits

§1. Ordinary Benefits for Private Employees

113. As has already been said, there are two types of benefits, depending on whether the claimant is affected by invalidity or inability. For invalidity, the claimant is entitled to the ordinary invalidity allowance. The benefit is paid monthly, and cannot be passed on to relatives after death. There is also a time limit: the benefit is paid for three years, and can be renewed for further periods of three years each upon application, provided the condition of invalidity still exists and considering any work the claimant has eventually carried out. After three consecutive renewals, the benefit is automatically confirmed. Invalidity allowance calculations are the same as for old-age pensions under the new contributive system. Invalids under 57 years of age have a benefit calculated on the basis of a coefficient relative to the age of 57: this method favours younger claimants.[63] If the benefit calculated using this method is lower than the legal minimum and the claimant falls into certain earnings categories, the amount is brought up to the minimum level. When retirement age is reached and the employment relation ceases, the invalidity allowance is changed into an old-age pension, provided that the contributions and insurance conditions have been met. The periods on invalidity allowance during which there has not been any work activity are counted for the purpose of the right to old-age pension but not of its amount. Beneficiaries who reach retirement age without the pension requirements continue to receive the invalidity allowance.

114. Claimants affected by inability receive the ordinary disability pension. This benefit may be passed on after death, pursuant to the regulations governing old-age pensions. Benefit is only awarded if the claimant gives up all rights to other earnings and benefits, and the claimant must apply to be removed from professional roles and societies. The pension has two elements: the invalidity allowance, plus an extra amount that depends on how long the claimant takes to reach retirement age (under the retributive system) or the age of 60 (under the contributive system). This calculation is made through a conventional increase of the contribution period; different methods of calculation will be applied, depending on whether the benefit is to be paid according to the old retributive or the new contributive system.[64]

115. The inability pension is incompatible with any earnings from self-employed or employed work in Italy or abroad, as with any other form of benefit targeted to earnings substitution or integration. Inability and invalidity benefits may not be added to pay-outs from INAIL for industrial accidents or professional diseases; but if the INAIL payments are less than the INPS benefit, the claimant also receives the difference between the two. When a claimant is working as an employee, predetermined reductions are made to the invalidity allowance amount. Furthermore, 70% of invalidity and inability benefits awarded (before the 1984 reforms) above the legal minimum may be added to self-employed earnings, and

63. *See* Part VIII of this study.
64. *See* Part VIII of this study.

any reductions in benefit may only reach a maximum of 30% of earnings. Finally, 50% of any invalidity pension may not be added to earnings from employment, up to parity with the earnings themselves.

116. Any claimant who cannot walk without the permanent help of an assistant, or who cannot carry out his/her normal day-to-day functions without constant help, is entitled to a monthly benefit for the personal and continuative assistance. The benefit may not be passed on after death.

§2. BENEFITS FOR PUBLIC EMPLOYEES

117. In public employment, benefits are calculated according to what entitlements the claimant would have had upon retirement; the benefit may not be more than 80% of the pension paid out after forty years' service. It can be handed over after death and is not compatible with earnings from any other type of work. The contributive system is used when calculating it. The pro-rata calculation (retributive system and contributive system) is used for those who started their working relationship before 1 January 1996.[65]

§3. PRIVILEGED BENEFITS

118. Compulsory general social insurance for invalidity, old-age, and survivors' pensions provides a special scheme for workers who have become invalid through service.[66] In particular, when the invalidity is in a direct causal relation with work, the claimant is entitled to a privileged invalidity allowance or to a privileged inability pension. The benefits, managed by INPS, have the same regime as the ordinary invalidity and inability benefits. The only difference is that entitlement to them is granted even when the usual minimum contributions and insurance requirements have not been met. When the claimant's death is directly caused by work, INPS pays a privileged pension to the survivors. Given that these benefits are specifically paid after professional risks, we shall speak more fully of them in the section dealing with industrial accidents and occupational diseases.[67]

---

65. *See* on this Part VIII of this study.
66. Article 6, Act No. 222 of 1984.
67. *See* Part VI of this study.

Part VI. Industrial Accidents and Occupational Diseases

Chapter 1. Field of Application

§1. Social Protection for Industrial Accidents and Occupational Diseases

119. Provision for the consequences of industrial accidents has always taken a prominent position among social insurance schemes: in the first place, because it is the oldest branch of social security in Italy. The first compulsory insurance scheme was introduced in 1898 and was confined in its scope to the industrial sector.[68] The insurance protection was extended to the agricultural sector in 1917. The scheme for the consequence of industrial diseases was, however, enacted only in 1929.[69] The importance of this provision in Italy's social insurance system is also linked to the fact that it provides the most generous benefits: the victims of industrial accidents and diseases are given a more favourable treatment than those disabled by other causes. Indeed, benefits are paid until recovery and are guaranteed even if the employer did not comply with the relevant contributions requirements ('principle of automatic payment of benefits', which is here fully operative). The reason for the privileged treatment rests on both the particular value that the legislator recognizes when working under a contract of employment and the greater hazard run at work than elsewhere. The root of this insurance is, however, traditionally traced in a basic transaction: the employer pays the contributions and benefits according to a limitation of his liability under tort law; the employees, on the other hand, obtain special provisions for the consequences of industrial accidents and diseases, irrespective of negligence, but accept a restoration for a lesser amount than that of the damage incurred.

120. The industrial accidents and diseases scheme is operative only in relation to dangerous activities (even though the definition of dangerous activities adopted covers the great majority of workers under a contract of employment); moreover, the financing of the scheme, as we shall see, is risk-related, while the benefits paid are basically of a compensatory nature. This shows how these provisions are still linked to private insurance principles, despite both the wording of Article 38 of the

68. Act No. 80 of 17 Mar. 1898.
69. Act of 13 May 1929.

Constitution, which envisages a comprehensive social security system designed to address the state of need and the intention of delivering more favourable treatment to the victims of industrial accidents and diseases over those disabled by other causes. An attempt at abandoning the vestiges of the risk-related approach is, however, embodied by the 'principle of automatic payment of benefits'. The present-day discipline of social insurance is laid down in the Decree Law of 30 June 1965, No. 1124; the legislation in the field of industrial accidents and diseases has remained, until recently, unchanged. In fact, case law has proved to be extremely important in adjusting the dated legislation to new situations. A reform was enacted by Legislative Decree No. 38/2000. This law made the following changes: (a) extended the insurance provisions to managers, certain self-employed, and to professional athletes; (b) covered accidents while travelling and the so-called biological damage; (c) set up a system for periodically updating and revising the list of specified industrial diseases.

§2. The Material Scope of Application

121. As regards the coverage of the insurance scheme, one has to make a distinction between the personal and material scopes of application.

Under the material scope of the scheme only dangerous activities are covered. In the industrial sector, the following is regarded as dangerous: work carried out through automatic, pressure, or thermal and electric machines; the activities that are subsidiary and complementary to work carried out through automatic, pressure, or thermal and electric machines; work carried out in plants where automatic, pressure, or thermal and electric machines are installed.

Moreover, twenty-eight specific activities (such as construction, draining, loading, and unloading and so forth) and those activities that are subsidiary and complementary to them have been declared dangerous by the law, independent of the presence of automatic machines.[70]

The concept of the automatic machine has been defined by case law: in particular, an automatic machine is considered any mechanism or set of mechanisms geared to obtain the highest output with the least effort, independent of the complexity, the dimension, and the kind of energy used. Automatic machines are regarded as dangerous because their functioning relies on an independent source of energy and cannot be directly controlled by the employee. This definition of dangerous work covers the great majority of dependent workers. In the agricultural sector all activities are regarded as dangerous; the notion of agricultural activity adopted in this area of legislation is particularly broad.

§3. The Personal Scope of Application

122. Under the personal scope of application, on the other hand, all the employees who carry out manual activity, all workers employed in plants where there are

70. *See* Presidential Decree No. 1124 of 30 Jun. 1965.

automatic machines, as well as works superintendents, home workers, and those employed in housework, are covered. Originally, the notion of 'manual activity' was used to ban automatically the white-collar workers from benefits; then, however, the technological changes and the introduction of new working patterns deprived this criterion of its value as far as the employees' classification is involved. At present, therefore, the concept of manual activity is interpreted in a very broad sense and it is used in relation to employees of any category in order to determine whether or not they are covered by insurance having regard to the work actually carried out. Legislative Decree No. 38 of 2000 has extended the coverage of insurance to managers, to professional athletes, and to a particular category of self-employed workers, whose relationship with the main contractor is characterized by coordination, continuity, and is prevalently personal.

123. Furthermore, the insurance is applied to categories of workers expressly listed, that is, to:

(a) apprentices;
(b) craftsmen;
(c) radiologists;
(d) salesmen;
(e) members of cooperative societies or of other societies and to the working members of social cooperatives;
(f) dockers companies;
(g) porters;
(h) sharecroppers and farmers;
(i) working profit sharers in associated partnerships;
(j) teleworkers and smart workers;
(l) riders.

Italian employees and craftsmen abroad are also covered.

124. Finally, insurance also covers persons who are not engaged in a formal employment relationship but are nonetheless exposed to the risk, that is:

(a) landowners and tenants;
(b) students and teachers;
(c) trainees;
(d) assisting relatives in the family business;
(e) unemployed engaged in public utility works;
(f) working convicts and their superintendents and instructors;
(g) working priests and members of religious orders;
(h) subjects aged between 18 and 67, who perform care work in the home, without pay and for one person only.

Chapter 2. Concept of Industrial Accident

§1. The Violent Cause

125. Entitlement to the insurance benefits in both the industrial and agricultural sectors is based on proof that the claimant suffers personal injury produced by violent cause during his employment. This definition contains three different elements:

(1) the violent cause;
(2) the employment risk;
(3) the personal injury.

126. The personal injury must be caused by a 'violent cause': that is to say, the injury must be produced by an event characterized by both abnormal energy and rapidity, here intended as intensity concentrated in a short lapse of time. This shows the preference granted by the system to traumatically caused disabilities. However, the violent cause may not be excluded in the hypothesis of the accident that produces deferred pathological effects, provided that the origin of the disease is rooted in a violent event. The classic example is that of the worker who develops pneumonia as a result of the breakage during the winter of a skylight in a furnace. The violent cause is constantly equalized in case law to the infection of bacteria or virus; as regards COVID19, the legislator has stated that this can be a violent cause covered by the industrial accident scheme.[71] The claimant must prove that the accident caused the injury. This, nevertheless, does not mean that it must be the sole cause of the injury; the accident can be a contributory cause, in connection with, for instance, a pre-existing condition. Two kinds of previous conditions are relevant here: the pre-existing causes of injury and the pre-existing causes of disability. The presence of the former worsens the injury caused by the accident at work; while the latter makes the disabilities resulting from the accident more serious. In the first case, the claimant is entitled to an assessment based on the aggregate of the respective degrees of disablement. In the hypothesis of pre-existing conditions of disability, on the other hand, a distinction has to be made: when the different disabilities are covered by the scheme, again the claimant has a right to an assessment based on the aggregate of the respective degrees of disablement; when the claimant's condition results in part from an extraneous cause not arising from an industrial accident, then the assessment is made on the basis of the reduced capacity for work determined by the pre-existing condition rather than on the basis of one's normal working capacity. The aggregation of the degrees of disablement, when it is allowed, rests on the principle that the total disability resulting from different events is greater than the sum of each disability taken separately. The question is more delicate when the industrial accident precedes other disabilities. The legislation allows the aggregation of the degrees of disablement only when the successive disabilities arise from an industrial accident.

71. Articles 26 and 42, Act No. 27/2020.

§2. The Employment Risk

127. As in all the industrial injury insurances, the accident must be connected with the employment. In particular, the accident must occur 'in occasion of employment'. The law does not require, therefore, a stringent causal link between the accident and the employment. However, the fact that the accident occurred at the normal place of work during the normal hours of work (i.e., the spatial and temporal elements) is regarded as not sufficient for a claim to be successful. The claimant has to show that the employment created a risk for him which is greater than, or at least different from, that to which he would have been subject as a member of the public (the so-called specific risk). According to this rule, claimants injured while carrying out trade union activities were covered, chiefly when these activities were concerned with terms and conditions of employment with the particular employer. As regards COVID-19 infection at work, there are categories of workers – that is health workers exposed to a high risk of contagion and workers assigned to duties that involve constant contact with the public – to whom, in the event of contagion, a 'simple presumption' can be applied with reference to the working origin of it (the 'simple presumption' can be, however, bypassed by a proof of the contrary); for all the other workers, it is necessary to prove that the infection occurred at work and not in private life.[72]

128. Accidents while travelling are also covered. Accidents while travelling are defined as those that happen when the worker is going from home to the workplace or vice versa. The most common types covered are: the worker has an accident somewhere along the only road he/she could take to get to work; or when he/she has to use special vehicles supplied by the employer; or when the victim has to transport heavy or bulky tools or equipment which impeded movement. Accidents while travelling have always been covered even when the connection with work was only an indirect one. This happened when accidents were caused by so-called traffic risks. In this way, a worker is covered when waiting along the road for a colleague who was to drive him/her to the workplace. In the same way, a worker who is going home for lunch because he/she could not use the company canteen for health reasons is also paid the industrial accident benefit.

Coverage for accidents while travelling was however finally provided for by Legislative Decree No. 38 of 2000. This law extended coverage to the following accidents: along the normal home-work-home route; on the road between two workplaces, if the worker works in two different places; between the workplace and the place where he/she takes his/her meal, when there is no company canteen. Coverage is not provided if the accident happens when a worker leaves the normal route for purposes unconnected with work or for purposes different from an act of force majeure, urgent and fundamental necessities and obligations set by criminal law. Nor are accidents covered when directly caused by alcohol or drug abuse, nor when the non-therapeutic use of drugs is involved. Insurance will not be involved if the worker is driving a vehicle for which he/she has no legal license.

72. In case of COVID-19 infection in occasion of employment, benefit is paid also for the period of quarantine or fiduciary home stay with abstention from work (Arts 26 and 42, Act No. 27/2020).

129. The intentional wrongdoing and negligence of the claimant are not by itself sufficient to bar entitlement to benefits. Thus, the worker is covered when the fault consists of carelessness, negligence, or inexperience. Accidents are not covered when the worker acts maliciously. There is no cover when the worker's negligence is not connected with the work to be carried out. This includes working while under the influence of alcohol. Accidents are not covered when the worker acts outside the scope of his/her employment. This is, for instance, the case when the worker plays with tools as a joke. These types of exclusions are known as 'chosen risk-related accidents': in these cases, the employee's intentional wrongdoing and negligence add or create a different risk to or from that arising from the employment.

§3. The Personal Injury

130. The notion of 'personal injury' does not cover all the adverse physical or mental consequences of the accidents, but only those that result in the employee's death or in his/her incapacity for work. More specifically, benefits are conferred for the hypothesis of: (a) temporary absolute incapacity of following the employee's regular occupation, which lasts more than three days; (b) permanent, absolute, or partial incapacity to work. The permanent partial incapacity, in particular, is covered only when it is over 6%: under this degree of disablement the loss of faculties resulting from the accident is deemed to be irrelevant by law. As regards the permanent incapacity, it is considered sufficient for the claimant to prove that the duration of his/her condition is unpredictable; there is no need to make predictions as to whether the loss of faculties will persist indefinitely.

131. Disabilities that do not spoil the employee's capacity for work, that is, the so-called biological injuries, were originally excluded from the insurance coverage. The notion of biological injuries embraces the damages caused to the person that does not necessarily involve one's own earning capacity. Disfigurement not accompanied by any actual loss of faculty, for example, was covered only when the claimant's appearance was such as to impair his/her possibilities to find a suitable occupation. Legislative Decree No. 38 of 23 February 2000 defines the biological injury as 'the loss of physical or mental faculties of the person, which can be legally assessed', is independent of the victim's earning capacity, and extends to it the coverage of public insurance. The degree of disablement is assessed in this case according to a specific list made by the INAIL and approved by ministerial decree; this list takes into consideration all the dynamic and relational aspects of the disablement. Benefits are then proportionate to the degree of disablement: the loss of faculties assessed between 6% and 15% is compensated by a lump sum; the 15% assessment and over is paid through annuity, which includes the compensation of the biological injury as well as that for the consequences of the injury, having regard to the claimant's earnings.

Chapter 3. Concept of Occupational Diseases

132. Cover for occupational diseases is accessory to that of industrial accidents: in other words, it is only applied to workers covered by the industrial accidents scheme. Up to 1988, occupational diseases were only covered if provided for in special lists. These lists are peremptory, and alongside the various diseases they state the various categories of employment where coverage is provided for. Occupational diseases are covered only when they are contracted 'while working at and because of' a particular type of activity listed. The lists also give the maximum lapse of time between the termination of the unhealthy occupation and the date on which the employee is treated as having developed the disease, for the disease to be regarded as causally linked with work. This was applied to both industrial and agricultural workers. The system just described is known as the 'scheduled diseases system'.

Italian law requires work to be the direct and determining cause of the disease, and not merely the occasion, as is the case with accidents. However, the causal link with work is presumed for the scheduled diseases, with no possibility of proving the contrary; which is to say that a worker has only to prove both that he/she is suffering from a disease included in the list and that he/she is working at one of the scheduled occupations. Italian courts have always interpreted the lists very broadly.

In 1988 the Constitutional Court,[73] in a change to its foregoing consolidated case law, said that the measures regarding occupational diseases were unconstitutional because they limited coverage to those listed in the tables. The Court also declared the maximum lapse of time required for the disease to be observed after the termination of unhealthy work unconstitutional. These decisions introduced a mixed system in Italy: as well as the listed diseases, other diseases, even when not listed as pertaining to types of occupation or when the onset happened later than the maximum period allowed, may be covered. For non-listed diseases, however, the worker must show that the illness has come on as a result of work. This proof, as has been said above, is not required in the case of listed diseases. In the same way as with workplace accidents, the right to cover is only granted when the worker's ability to work is reduced by more than 6%.[74]

133. A special law[75] deals with silicosis and asbestosis. The first of these diseases is brought about by inhalation of silicon oxide powder, the second by inhalation of asbestos powder. Italian law does not define these diseases, and leaves diagnosis up to a competent doctor. The right to insurance coverage is provided even when these diseases are contracted merely 'on occasion' of the relevant specific occupations and are not necessarily causally linked to them. Compensation is paid out even when silicosis and asbestosis are associated with other breathing and cardiovascular diseases.

134. Article 10 of Legislative Decree No. 38 of 2000, is a possible answer to the problem of periodically updating the occupational diseases lists. In particular,

73. Constitutional Court, 18 Feb. 1988, No. 179; Constitutional Court, 25 Feb. 1988, No. 206.
74. *See* Constitutional Court, 30 May 1977, No. 93.
75. Act No. 780 of 1975.

this law has provided for the setting up of a scientific board to elaborate and revise the lists. Any modifications or integration the board proposes must then be approved by a ministerial decree, after the most representative trade unions of the category have been heard. Article 10 was implemented by Ministerial Decree on 27 April 2004: the Decree provided a new and much more comprehensive list of occupational diseases, which must be compulsorily denounced to INAIL; the diseases are now classified on the basis of both the risk agents and the degree of risk attached to the working activities performed.

Chapter 4. Medical Care

135. In the event of industrial accidents or occupational diseases, workers have the right to healthcare and benefits. Health coverage for workers who are victims of accidents or of occupational diseases is paid by the NHS. This consists of both the necessary medical and surgical care for the whole period of temporary disability and the healthcare required after recovery to regain the ability to work. Even when returning to work is regarded as impossible, that is, when the worker's health has been permanently and irreparably damaged, healthcare is continued, provided that the worker's situation deserves particular attention. In the event of refusal, even without reasonable cause, of medical treatment as prescribed by the medical authority, benefits are still paid. A former law, which required workers to continue with healthcare in order to receive benefits, was implicitly revoked with the reform of the Health Service in 1978.[76] Article 1 of the 1978 law states that the patient's dignity and freedom must not be impaired when taking care of his/her mental and physical health.

Prosthesis is still provided by the INAIL, notwithstanding the institution of the NHS; the INAIL, however, can make conventions with the Health Service on this issue. The INAIL is responsible for ascertaining and issuing certificates on the medical situation of workers who are victims of industrial accidents and diseases and to grant, according to conventions stipulated with the regional authorities, the first surgical treatment. INAIL is also entrusted with a few tasks in the area of prevention: it is responsible for promoting solutions, also at a legislative level, in order to decrease the rates of industrial accidents and diseases; moreover, INAIL takes part in the observatory existing at the Ministry of Labour, which is in charge of the analysis of the dangerous activities and of the risk factors at work. Finally, the INAIL supplies the technical and informatics support to the SINP: the service was set up by the recent Legislative Decree No. 81 of 2008 and it is composed of the Employment Health and Social Policy Ministry, the Home Office, local authorities, the INAIL, with the contribution of the National Council of Economy and Employment.

76. Act No. 833 of 1978.

Chapter 5. Absolute and Specific Temporary Inability

136. The provision of cash benefits is entrusted to INAIL. Benefits are differentiated according to whether the disease is temporary or permanent. The right to benefits is provided even when the employer has not paid insurance contributions. Indeed, in cases such as this, the principle of the 'automatic payment of benefits' is fully applied. The right to cover is not conditioned on a minimum of contributions previously paid. Benefits are dependent upon the claimant's salary level. The right to benefits has a prescription term of three years. Any benefits paid out for industrial accidents or occupational disease cannot be cumulated with other pensions, benefits, or war pensions: the claimant may choose the most favourable benefit to be paid. The permanent invalidity benefit may not be cumulated with disability pensions or invalidity benefits paid out for the same invalidity; the benefits and pensions that exceed the amount of the permanent invalidity benefit are paid, however. The permanent invalidity benefit can, on the other hand, be cumulated with old-age pensions.

137. In the case of absolute and specific temporary inability, the industrial worker has the right to an earning-related daily allowance, while the agricultural worker is paid a flat-rate benefit. The term 'absolute and specific temporary inability' means temporary but total psychic or physical incapacity to carry out one's job. The daily allowance is paid from the fourth day after the accident happened or the disease began. The allowance is paid as long as the disability lasts. The allowance amounts to 60% of pay; if the inability continues after ninety days (not necessarily consecutive), the allowance goes up to 75% of pay. In industry, the allowance is calculated according to the wages (either in money or in kind) the worker was earning over the twelve months previous to the accident.

During the three days waiting period, the allowance is paid by the employer: the worker is paid his/her entire wage for the day of the accident or the day of the onset of the occupational disease; for the next three days, he/she receives 60% of wages.

It must be pointed out that most collective bargaining contracts set down an integration of the allowance up to the full wage, for a period of time proportional to the worker's years of service. Normally, the indemnity is paid by the employer, who then applies for a reimbursement from INAIL.

Chapter 6. Permanent Disability

138. According to Legislative Decree No. 38/2000, in the event of permanent disability, the claimant has the right to a benefit that covers him for both the biological damage and the working ability reduction. By 'generic permanent disability' is meant a permanent inability of the claimant to carry out any type of work. The benefit provides total coverage of the biological damage when the inability is greater than or equal to 6%. This part of the benefit is calculated according to the degrees of disablement, irrespective of the claimant's wage level. It is paid out in a lump sum when the disablement is less than 16%, and as an allowance when it is 16% or more. When damage is greater than or equal to 16%, the allowance is made up with a benefit to compensate for the loss of earnings due to the accident or occupational disease. This benefit is calculated on the basis of the claimant's wages and degree of invalidity; account is kept of the type of work normally carried out by the claimant and of how difficult it would be to re-deploy him/her. When calculating the amount of the integrative benefit, minimum and maximum wage levels are applied, which are reviewed annually. The system of calculation is based on the tariffs of the prescribed degree of disablement approved by the Employment Ministry. The amount paid out may be revised according to any increase or decrease in the claimant's ability to work or to any change in his health conditions. If the claimant's health conditions worsen, the benefit can be recalculated only when this is due to the accident that caused the benefit to be awarded. However, any review must take place within ten years from the first benefit assessment for industrial accidents, or fifteen years for occupational diseases.

Chapter 7. The Mobility Allowance

139. Claimants who are victims of industrial accidents or occupational diseases are also entitled to claim other benefits. One of these is the 'mobility allowance'. It is paid out to workers in receipt of benefits for a disability of 100% who require continuous assistance to carry out a normal life.

Another benefit is that paid out to workers affected by asbestosis or silicosis who have voluntarily left an employment connected with the disease (the so-called re-deployment allowance). In order to obtain this benefit, the level of permanent disability must not be more than 80%. The amount of benefit varies according to whether the claimant is unemployed or not.

The final benefit we wish to mention here is the 'inability to work allowance'. This is paid to those whose disability is such that they cannot be re-deployed.

Chapter 8. Survivors' Benefits

140. If an accident or occupational disease causes the death of the worker, the surviving relatives are entitled to an allowance of 100% of his/her annual normal wages. The allowance is paid to the deceased worker's spouse, sons, and daughters; if there are not any of these, it is paid to parents, sisters, and brothers. The spouse is entitled to 60% of the original benefit until he/she dies or remarries. Each son and daughter is entitled to 20% of the original benefit if their right concurs with the spouse's; otherwise they are entitled to 40% of the original benefit. When there is only one child, the amount is raised to 70% of the original benefit. The allowance is paid to the children up to 18 years of age, or 21 if they are still studying, or 26 if they are at university. If they are disabled, there is no upper age limit. The rights of legitimate children are extended to: natural or adopted children; descendants, if they were under the care of the deceased, provided they have lost both parents or their parents are unable to work; foster-children; and children born within three-hundred days of the death of the worker. Parents, brothers, and sisters have a right to 15% of the original benefit, provided that they were living with the deceased worker and were under his/her care. Brothers and sisters receive benefits under the same conditions as children. Overall benefits must not be more than the deceased's wage, nor less than 60% of it. If the calculated benefit is more than 100% of the deceased's wage, each claimant shall have his/her benefit proportionally reduced. Benefits paid to survivors in the event of death due to an industrial accident or occupational disease may be cumulated to the survivors' pension paid out by INPS.

141. Survivors are also entitled to payments for reimbursement of funeral charges. A special monthly allowance is paid to survivors when the death of a claimant in receipt of permanent disability allowance is not due to an industrial accident or occupational disease. This allowance is only payable when the degree of disability of the deceased was greater than 65%.

Chapter 9. Prevention

142. In the Italian system, the relationship between compensatory measures and preventive provisions has long been unbalanced in favour of compensatory measures. During the last ten years, however, there has been a shift in legislation towards safety at work and prevention of injuries, following the European Union Directives. These directives have been implemented by the Legislative Decree No. 626 of 1994 in first place and then by Legislative Decree No. 81 of 2008 (as modified by Legislative Decree No. 106/2009 and Legislative Decree No. 151/2015), that is to say, the Recast Act on Health and Safety at Work.[77] Under these laws, which address both dependent and self-employed workers, all employers are obliged: to evaluate the occupational risks, especially in the choice of work equipment and the fitting-out of workplaces, and to make provision for adequate protective and preventive services; to evaluate the stress level work-linked; to inform and consult workers and allow them to take part in discussions on all questions relating to safety and health at work; to ensure that each worker receives adequate safety and health training throughout the period of employment; to designate responsibility for protection and prevention of occupational risks. Furthermore, workers are entitled to have a representative with specific responsibility for health and safety at work. The law also ensures the presence within the undertaking of a service of medical supervision. On the other hand, workers are asked to cooperate in fulfilling any requirements imposed for the protection of health and safety and in enabling the employer to ensure that the working environment and working conditions are safe and pose no risks.

77. *See also*: Art. 2087, Civil Code; Art. 9, Act No. 300 of 20 May 1970; Law Decree No. 242/1996; Act No. 123/2007.

Chapter 10. Employer's Civil Liability

143. Italian law expressly exonerates the employer from civil liability derived from the industrial accident or occupational disease of his worker. The consequence of this is that workers cannot obtain compensation from their employers over and above the social insurance amounts. This is even the case when an industrial accident happens or occupational disease breaks out through the employer's fault. This limit is important when one considers that benefits, as we have shown above, are contained below certain maximum levels. This exoneration only applies, obviously, within the objective and subjective scope of the social insurance scheme. Outside the scope of social insurance, the precepts of ordinary civil or tort law continue to be applied. Exoneration, however, is not applied when a criminal or civil court states that the industrial accident or the occupational disease has occurred as a consequence of a prosecutable offence committed by the employer or one of his/ her employees. In this regard, we should point out that in the Italian system almost all examples of industrial accidents and occupational diseases are the consequence of a prosecutable offence committed by the employer. So the area of exoneration is in fact extremely limited.

Chapter 11. The Financing of the Scheme

144. Contribution, the collection of which is entrusted to the INAIL, is paid exclusively by employers. The contribution varies on the basis of the occupational sector's accident record. The INAIL classifies to this end the different industries or firms according to the criterion of the 'average national risk'. Moreover, the contribution is also linked to every single industry or firm's accident record that is the so-called pondered risk. A supplementary contribution is due by those employers whose activities engender the risk of silicosis and asbestosis. Contribution is calculated on the basis of the total wage effectively paid to employees. The contribution prescription term is five years.

145. Special provisions are made for apprentices: in the industrial and commercial sectors, the contribution is paid at a reduced rate; in the handicraft sector, the contribution is fixed according to specific regional conventions. In the agricultural sector, the contribution is paid by the landowner; the contribution rate is fixed by ministerial decree. The sharecroppers and tenants, on the other hand, are required to pay a contribution calculated on the basis of their annual profits. Finally, the self-employed are also charged with a contribution equivalent to a prescribed proportion of their annual profits.

146. In the Italian system, therefore, risks are not pooled: each industry or firm continues to bear part of its own accident costs. The main argument for relating the financial responsibility of the industry or firm to the risks engendered by its activities rests on the conviction that this option acts as an incentive to both safety and prevention of injuries. Furthermore, this system is trusted to avoid the phenomenon of low-risk industry subsidizing high-risk industry, which can in turn cause a price distortion.

Chapter 12. The Procedure

147. The victim or someone acting on his/her behalf must give notice of the accident as soon as possible to the employer: more specifically, in case of industrial injury the employee is required to inform the employer immediately; in the hypothesis of occupational disease, notice must be given within fifteen days. In the event of non-compliance with these obligations, the claimant may lose the social insurance benefits: indeed, the claimant has no right to benefits for the days when the employer had no knowledge of the event; moreover, there is a three-year time limit for declaration. The employer, on the other hand, must give notice of the accident within two days and of the occupational disease within five days to the INAIL, unless the prognosis is three days or less; the communication of the employer must contain a factual account of the circumstances and a detailed description of the injuries. The INAIL, on receipt of the appropriate notice or once it has anyhow gained knowledge of the event, starts a procedure geared to verify the coverage of insurance and to assess the degree of the disablement.

148. The employee has the onus of proving that the accident arose during work or that the non-scheduled disease was caused by his/her employment. There exists in our system a procedure, however, the so-called magistrate inquiry, geared to facilitate the proof of the connection between the employment and the accident occurred. In cases of death or disablement of duration of over thirty days, the competent public authorities (police superintendent or mayor of the town), on receipt of the appropriate notice from the employer, must transmit a copy of the inquiry to the magistrate. The magistrate starts an inquiry within four days in order to ascertain: the existence of any liability; the nature of the work carried out by the employee; the factual circumstances of the accident or of the occupational disease; the causes, the nature, and the degree of the disablement; the situation and the domestic conditions of the claimant. A medical practitioner appointed by the magistrate can take part in the inquiry, which is carried out in the presence of all the parties involved. The outcome of the inquiry is entered in minutes and this is brought to the attention of the public prosecutor in order to ascertain the existence of grounds for a criminal proceeding. The minutes of the magistrate's inquiry have the value of a technical consultation and as such they can be used in the legal proceedings eventually started.

Chapter 13. Industrial Accidents and Occupational Diseases in the Invalidity Pensions Scheme

149. The compulsory general insurance scheme for invalidity, old-age, and survivors provides a special system that covers workers who have become invalid because of their employment.[78] In particular, when the invalidity is a direct result of work, the claimant has a right to a privileged invalidity allowance or to a privileged inability pension. The allowance is paid out to any worker whose work capacity, in suitable occupations in relation to his specific abilities, is reduced permanently, through a mental or physical disease, to less than a third. The pension is paid to a worker who, because of mental or physical handicap, is permanently unable to carry out any work. The benefits regime under this scheme, which is run by INPS, is the same as for ordinary invalidity benefits and disability pensions.[79] The only difference is that workers have a right to these benefits, even if they have not fulfilled the contributions and insurance requirements. These benefits may not be cumulated with the benefits paid by the industrial accidents and occupational diseases insurance or with the benefits that are paid with continuity by social assistance or social insurance schemes. When the death of the claimant has a direct causal link with the work, INPS also pays the privileged survivors' pension.[80] This pension may not be cumulated with the survivors' benefits paid out by INAIL or with any other similar payment made by a social insurance scheme.

78. Article 6, Act No. 222 of 1984.
79. For details, *see* Part V of this study.
80. *See* Part V of this study.

Part VII. Unemployment

Chapter 1. Unemployment Benefit

§1. Field of Application

150. Social protection for the unemployed finds its roots, within the Italian social security system, in Articles 38, 4, and 35 of the Constitutional Charter. According to Article 38 of the Constitution, second paragraph, the intervention of the social security provisions is activated when there is a shortage of work on the market. This rule conditions the public intervention to the presence of a situation of involuntary unemployment. The claimant's inactivity, in other words, must depend on lack of work with reference to his/her job position on the labour market rather than on his/her attitude towards work: those who are voluntarily unemployed are therefore banned from benefits. On the other hand, those who are unable to work for health reasons are protected under the sickness pay provisions. Article 38 regards the social security provisions for the unemployed essentially as an income maintenance system.

151. However, the social security system for the unemployed is also based on Article 4, first paragraph and Article 35, first paragraph of the Constitution. These norms recognize the right to work of all citizens. Article 38, on the one hand, and Articles 4 and 35, on the other, can be considered as complementary: in fact, the situation of unemployment is caused by a non-implementation of the right to work. Moreover, the principal target of the social security system is that of removing the causes of distress themselves, as well as their effects: in the hypothesis of unemployment, therefore, social protection aims in the first place at restoring the worker to his/her job, and in the meantime at providing him/her with an income. The social security system envisaged by the Constitutional Charter, therefore, has been conceived to provide the unemployed with both income and occupational protection: the claimant is granted an income under Article 38, adequate to the necessities of life with a view to attenuate the effects of unemployment. Furthermore, as provided for by Articles 4 and 35, the social protection system attempts at finding new jobs for the unemployed, thus removing the causes of distress. This definition of the social protection system for the unemployed includes: unemployment benefit and CIG-CIGS (ISCRO, for the self-employed).[81]

81. Special unemployment benefits and short time earning funds are also provided for agricultural workers.

152. The unemployment benefit scheme (NASPI) covers all the workers who are at least 14 years old and who are gainfully employed under a contract of service. The major exclusions from NASPI are represented by public employees (but those employed with a temporary contract are however included).

Thirteen weeks of contributions during the four years before the beginning of unemployment is required for benefit entitlement.[82]

§2. Amount of the Benefit

153. Unemployment benefits are income-related. The benefit amount is 75% of the average earned salary of the four years prior to the beginning of the period of unemployment, if the salary is inferior to EUR 1,227.55 a month (index-linked, annually); if the monthly salary is higher than the aforementioned amount, the benefit is equal to 75% of the amount in question, increased by a sum equal to 25% of the differential between the monthly salary and this amount. Benefit, which is not laughable, cannot in any case exceed the maximum monthly amount of EUR 1,335.40 (index-linked annually). The benefit amount, however, is progressively reduced by 3% per month from the first day of the sixth month of use (of the eighth for unemployed over 54 years of age). Increases are available for dependents.

The benefit is paid monthly for a number of weeks equal to half the contribution weeks of the last four years; for the purpose of calculating benefit duration, the contribution periods that have already given rise to the payment of unemployment benefit are not calculated. Benefits cannot be paid during the first seven days in any one period of interruption of employment ('waiting days'). A final element in this appraisal of the treatment of claimants under the NASPI is represented by the credit of contributions, which can count for the entitlement and the amount of pensions; there is, however, a ceiling to the amount of notional contributions recognized and this may reduce the pension amount.

§3. Conditions

154. The benefit is paid to those who are involuntarily unemployed. It is claimed at the INPS. The involuntary nature of unemployment has to be shown by the claimant through his/her declaration of availability to work; this is automatically presented with the claim for benefit. The declaration of immediate availability is then transmitted by the INPS to the National Agency for Active Labour Policies (ANPAL), for the purpose of being included in the national informatics system of the active labour policies. On the basis of the information provided at the time of registration, the unemployed are assigned to a profiling class (periodically updated), according to an automated data processing procedure, in order to evaluate their level of employability. Claimants are then required to contact the job centres within fifteen days from the date of application; failing that, they are summoned by the employment centre. At that time, a personalized services agreement is drawn up, in

82. Law Decree No. 22/2015, as modified by Art. 1 para. 221, Act No. 234/2021.

which the employee undertakes to participate in initiatives and laboratories for the strengthening of competences in the active search for work, for training opportunities and to accept appropriate offers of work. The appropriate work offer is proposed by the ANPAL, on the basis of: consistency with the experiences and skills gained; distance from home and transfer times by public transport; duration of unemployment; level of pay offered, which must be at least 20% higher than the allowance received in the previous month (which is anyway progressively reduced by 3% per month from the first day of the sixth month of use, as we already wrote). The penalty for failing to comply with the personalized services agreement is the loss of unemployment benefits, for a part or for the whole, depending on the kind and on the reiteration of the infractions committed.[83]

Finally, the claimant who voluntarily leaves his/her employment without a just cause or who consensual terminate the working relationship is regarded as being voluntarily unemployed and he/she will thus be banned from benefits.

155. The unemployed under NASPI, whose unemployment lasts more than four months, receive on request a sum called 'individual reinsertion check', which is graded according to the personal employability profile; this sum can be spent at public or private (authorized) job centres. The 'individual reinsertion check' differs from the personalized services agreement, which is suspended for the period of the check, for the intensity of services provided, to which the tutorial tool is essential. The job centre can be paid with the 'check' only once the unemployed has found a job. The GOL programme (Workers Employability Guarantee) also addresses the NASPI recipients: this is a PNRR (Recovery and Resilience Plan in the ambit of Next Generation EU) scheme geared to the reintegration into the labour market of the unemployed.[84]

156. Benefit is suspended if the claimant becomes employed in a temporary work not longer than six months. If the income derived from an employment relationship (subordinate or quasi-subordinate) assumed by the recipient of the benefits is lower than the minimum income excluded from taxation, NASPI is maintained, naturally to a reduced extent. On the other hand, a worker with two part-time relationships who loses one and whose income corresponds to a gross tax equal to or less than the income tax deductions may apply for a reduced unemployment benefit. The NASPI is also reduced: when the recipient of the indemnity carries out ancillary work activities with an annual income of between EUR 3,000 and EUR 7,000; in the event of an intermittent employment contract, with or without the obligation to answer the call, where the income produced allows the unemployment status to be maintained. At the same time, the unemployed who undertakes an autonomous or individual business activity, from which derives an income that corresponds to a gross tax equal to or less than the income tax deductions, keeps

83. Law Decree No. 150/2015.
84. Article 1 para. 324, Act No. 234/2021.

NASPI at a reduced amount.[85] The pay received by the occasional employee is tax exempt and does not affect the state of unemployment.[86]

§4. FINANCING

157. NASPI is financed by: ordinary contributions paid by employers; an additional 1.4% contribution on temporary contracts; a further one-off contribution, the so-called dismissal fee, equal to 41% of the initial monthly unemployment benefit, for every twelve months of company seniority in the last three years, triplicable in case of collective dismissals not supported by a company agreement.[87]

§5. UNEMPLOYMENT BENEFIT FOR THE SO-CALLED PARA-EMPLOYEES

158. According to Act No. 81/2017, workers having a co-ordinate and continuative relationship with a particular company or institution (the so-called para-employees) and project workers, enrolled in the 'Fourth Fund' of the INPS, benefit of a special unemployment provision called 'DIS-COLL' (Unemployment Benefit for 'Para-Employees'). DIS-COLL also covers university grant holders and PhD students with scholarship who become unemployed.

In order to get the benefit, para-employees and project workers, who have to be involuntarily unemployed, must have at least one month contributions accrued in the period that goes from 1 January of the previous calendar year up to the dismissal.[88] Benefit amount is calculated as for the NASPI, in relation to taxable income deriving from relationships of collaboration during the year in which unemployment occurred and during the previous calendar year. Benefit is paid, monthly, for a number of months equal to the contribution weeks of the period from the 1 January of the previous calendar year up to the event of cessation of work; benefit cannot in any case exceed the maximum duration of twelve months.[89] Here too the seven days waiting period and the décalage of the benefit from the sixth month are applied. DIS-COLL gives entitlement to notional contributions, although partially. The same conditions as NASPI as regards availability to work are applied. Para-employees and project workers, grant holders and PhD students with scholarship, who have the right to receive DIS-COLL, as well as CEO and auditors (registered exclusively in the 'Fourth Fund' of the INPS), who do not have this right, are required to pay contributions for the financing of the benefit.

85. Law Decree No. 150/2015.
86. Article 54, para. 4, Act No. 96/2017.
87. Article 2, paras 31–35, Act No. 92/2012; Art. 1, para. 250, Act No. 228/2012.
88. Article 2 para. 1, Decree No. 101/2019.
89. Article 1 para. 223, Act No. 234/2021.

Chapter 2. Short-Time Earning Funds

§1. Field of Application

159. This benefit was introduced in our system during the Second World War. Since then, the CIG-CIGS have gone through a radical evolution. They had originally been conceived as an instrument to provide temporarily redundant workers with an income for the working hours lost as a result of a diminution in the requirements of the employer's business. In principle, the peculiar feature of the short-time earning funds is, therefore, that the benefit is paid only when there still formally exists a contract of employment. It is no longer paid when workers are dismissed or made redundant. Nonetheless, the short-time earning funds took up several functions during the years, last but not least that of providing the unemployed with an income.

160. At the origin, the benefit was meant to intervene only in the case of 'involuntary', 'temporary' events that caused a suspension or reduction of the firm's production (such as failure of power supply, equipment failure, natural disasters). Very soon, however, the intervention was also provided for situations of contractions of the enterprise's activity that were no longer due to an involuntary event, but to managerial choices. On the other hand, the causes of the suspension/reduction ceased to be transitory. The intervention started to be allowed for an indefinite duration, even when the recovery of the enterprise was compromised. Moreover, laws passed ad hoc postponed the benefit duration for particular sectors or for specific enterprises. Furthermore, special provisions were enacted, which left behind the traditional requirements of the event. In some cases workers were kept in CIGS even for ten years or more. In other situations the benefit was allowed for an indefinite duration for workers of enterprises that had gone bankrupt and had no hope of recovery. The short-time earning funds thus became another benefit for the unemployed: the benefit was in principle paid to temporarily redundant people, but most of the time these persons would never come back to work because their jobs did not exist any longer. Therefore, this benefit quite often ended up being a mere prelude to redundancies.

161. A considerable effort to bring back to life the requirements of the 'temporariness' of the event and of the 'certainty' of the productive recovery of the enterprise was made by the legislator in 1991.[90] The reform was, however, followed by a series of temporary provisions geared to postpone benefits duration in various specific situations, to extend the validity of the special interventions, and to introduce new ad hoc interventions of the short-time earning funds.[91] Most of these provisions were still in force, despite the alleged temporariness, when Act No. 92/2012,

90. Act No. 223/1991.
91. *See e.g.*, Arts 6, 7, and 8, Act No. 236/1993; Art. 5, Act No. 451/1994; Art. 1, Act No. 56/1994; Art. 2, Act No. 460/1992; Act No. 402/1996; Act No. 608/1996; Act No. 662/1996; Act No. 135/1997; Act No. 52/1998; Act No. 176/1998; Act No. 251/1998; Art. 81, Act No. 448/1998; Art. 62, Act No.

first, and, above all, Law Decree No. 148/2015 finally reformed CIG-CIGS. The main changes were: the creation of occupational CIG-CIGS for the enterprises excluded by the discipline of public CIG-CIGS; the re-introduction of a definite duration for the different interventions; the rationalization of the general discipline of CIG-CIGS. Indeed, in a single legal text, that is Law Decree No. 148/2015, the rules of ordinary and extraordinary CIG-CIGS for the industrial and construction sectors and of occupational CIG-CIGS are given. Finally, a further regulatory text, Article 1 paragraphs 192–257 of Act No. 234/2021 (amended by Article 23, Law Decree No. 4/2022), modifies the consolidated text of 2015: the attempt, basic, is at reorganizing the matter. These provisions, however, also move in the wake of the existing situation and do not manage to rationalize the whole world of special provisions, which still survives despite three attempts to reform.

162. The present-day normative still fully reflects the functional complexity of the Institute. Indeed, alongside the general normative, which includes the discipline for workers of the industrial, agricultural, and construction sectors, there are yet special provisions enacted in order to face the crises affecting specific undertakings or particular sectors of the economy; again, there is a hypothesis of exceptions to the general discipline.

We shall, however, concentrate on the general discipline.

163. Under this normative, there are two different types of intervention, depending on the kind of crisis that affects the enterprise: the 'ordinary' (CIG) and the 'extraordinary' (CIGS) interventions. The former is reserved for a reduction or suspension of the enterprise activity due to either 'transitory involuntary events which cannot be imputed to the employers or to the workers (here included seasonal elements)' or 'cyclic downturns'. The latter concerns reductions or suspension of productive activities due to the enterprise's 'crisis' (excluded the plant shut-down) or 'reorganization' and solidarity contracts; the extraordinary intervention is also allowed when the employer is submitted to the procedure of extraordinary administration. 'Reorganization' may now also concern transition processes identified and regulated by a decree of the Minister of Labour and Social Policies, after consulting the Minister of Economic Development; the finalization of the programme, aimed at a substantial occupational recovery of the staff involved in the suspensions or reductions in working hours, can also take place in terms of professional requalification and skills enhancement.[92] The defensive solidarity contract useful for benefits intervention establishes a reduction of working time in order to avoid redundancies.

164. The recipients of the ordinary intervention are: industrial manufacturing, transport, mining, plant installation, production and distribution of energy, water

---

488/1999; Arts 45, 46, Act No. 144/1999; Art. 78, Act No. 388/2000. *See also* Art. 2, Act No. 248/2001; Art. 1, para. 521, Act No. 244/2007. Finally, *see* Acts No. 2 and No. 33 of 2009.

92. Until 2023, within 'reorganization' there also is included the so-called expansive solidarity contract: in support of the business development program, the expansion contract allows companies to introduce new professional skills, simultaneously launching a retraining process for existing staff, aimed at updating individual and collective skills.

and gas companies; production and labour cooperatives that carry out work activities similar to that of the workers of industrial enterprises; enterprises of the forest, forestry and tobacco industries; agricultural and livestock cooperatives and their consortia that carry out processing, manipulation and marketing of their own agricultural products for employees with permanent employment contracts only; companies involved in the rental and distribution of films and the development and printing of motion picture film; industrial companies for the pressing of olives on behalf of third parties; companies producing ready-mix concrete; companies involved in electrical and telephone systems; companies involved in railway superstructures; industrial enterprises of public bodies, except in the case in which the capital is wholly publicly owned; industrial and artisan construction and related companies; industrial companies engaged in the excavation and/or processing of stone material; artisan businesses that carry out excavation and processing of stone materials, except for those that carry out this processing activity in laboratories with structures and organization distinct from the excavation activity. On the other hand, following the 2021 reform, the general discipline of the extraordinary intervention applies to all employers with over fifteen employees and, regardless of the number of employees, to air transport companies and airport management and derivative companies, as well as airport system companies.

165. Benefits are paid to all those employees, here included apprentices and home workers, who have accrued at least thirty days of effective work in the productive unit for which the firm requires the intervention; this condition does not operate for the ordinary intervention in the industrial sector due to transitory involuntary events which cannot be imputed to the employers or to the workers. Finally, managers are excluded from coverage.

§2. Amount of the Benefit

166. The short-time earning funds pay the workers 80% of the salary lost as a result of the reduction/suspension (within a threshold based on previous earnings and annually revalued). The benefit is subject to tax and social security contributions (at a reduced rate). Claimants have a right to the crediting of contributions, which can count for the entitlement and the amount of pensions. They are also entitled to family allowances. The time spent on benefit is taken into consideration for the purpose of the amount of severance payments of the maternity and sickness benefits.

167. The 'ordinary' benefit's maximum duration is thirteen weeks, which can, however, be extended from a period of three months up to a maximum of fifty-two weeks. To obtain a new intervention, after fifty-two consecutive weeks of use in the same productive unit, however, a period of at least fifty-two weeks of working activity should pass. Moreover, benefit relating to several non-consecutive periods cannot exceed a total of fifty-two weeks in a two-year period. The two limits just mentioned do not apply to supplementary measures determined by objectively unavoidable events. Finally, the hours of ordinary short-time intervention exceeding the limit of one-third of the ordinary hours that can be worked in the two-year period cannot be authorized; this limit is calculated in relation to all the workers of the productive unit who are on average employed in the semester before the intervention.

The 'extraordinary' benefit for the enterprise's crisis is paid for a maximum of twelve months (even non-continuous) in a five-year period; while that for reorganization or solidarity contracts is paid for a maximum of twenty-four months (even non-continuous) in a five-year period. Furthermore, a new authorization for a company crisis cannot be granted before a period of two-thirds of that relating to the previous intervention has expired. For the solidarity contract, up to thirty-six months of duration can be reached, provided the cumulative ceiling is not exceeded.[93] Lastly, in the hypothesis of enterprise reorganization or crisis, job suspension can be authorized only up to 80% of the ordinary hours that can be worked in the productive unit, in the time frame provided by the authorized programme.

All these benefits cannot, however, have a duration superior to twenty-four months within a five-year period, whatever kind of intervention is allowed. This limit can be partially waived in the hypothesis of contracts of solidarity.[94]

168. The new 2021 regulation of conditionality focuses heavily on the strengthening of active labour market policies towards the recipients of extraordinary wage subsidies (both at the expense of the public system and of bilateralism), through training or retraining initiatives, also with the intervention of occupational interprofessional funds: failure to participate, without justified reason, in the training initiatives will result in penalties ranging from benefit reduction up to cancellation of the same. Short-time benefits are just suspended (not withdrawn) in case of recipients' work activities. The CIGS recipients due to the enterprise's 'crisis' or 'reorganization' receive on request, like the NASPI recipients, a sum called 'individual reinsertion check', which is graded according to the personal employability profile; this sum can be spent at public or private (authorized) job centres. The 'individual reinsertion check' is characterized by the intensity of services provided, to which the tutorial tool is essential. The job centre can be paid with the 'check' only once the recipient has found a job. The GOL programme (Workers Employability Guarantee) also addresses the short-time earning benefits recipients: this is a PNRR (Recovery and Resilience Plan in the ambit of Next Generation EU) scheme geared to the reintegration into the labour market. These provisions on availability to work have the purpose of targeting social benefits to an active employment policy, implementing Article 4 of the Constitution, which provides for the right to work and requires the state to promote the conditions that make it effective.

---

93. For 'reorganization' linked to the 'expansive solidarity contract', the intervention can last up to eighteen months.
94. There are exceptions to this limit also in relation to 'expansive solidarity contract' as well as for industrial and artisan construction companies and the like, for industrial companies carrying out the excavation and/or processing of stone material and for artisan companies that carry out excavation and processing activities of stone materials.

§3. Procedures and Financing

169. The benefit is demanded by the employer through an administrative procedure, after trade-union consultation. This consultation has to concern the characteristics and the reasons of the productive contraction and the number of workers to be put on short time. The concession of the 'ordinary' short-time earning funds and of its extensions is authorized by the INPS. The extraordinary intervention and its extensions, on the other hand, are authorized by the Ministry of Employment. The employer has to present to this end an application form, concurrently and electronically, to the INPS, the Ministry of Employment and the territorial Labour directorates. The application must contain a project geared to the recovery of the enterprise.

170. The choice of workers to be put on short time is left to the agreement that may be reached between the employer and trade unions through the consultation procedure. Priority is given to rotation of the intervention throughout all the workers involved in the same jobs, although this criterion is not compulsory. The employer who breaches the agreement providing for rotation is penalized through an increase of his/her contributions to the scheme.

171. The benefit is mainly financed through taxation. A growing share of the cost is, however, charged to the employers included in the scheme, through contributions; the firms who apply for short-time earning funds are requested to pay an additional contribution. From 2025, employers who have not requested benefits for at least twenty-four months are rewarded with the reduction of the additional contribution. Workers covered by the scheme also pay a limited contribution.

§4. Occupational CIG-CIGS

172. Occupational CIG-CIGS are an attempt at extending the coverage of this institute to those workers who are not protected by the public scheme. According to Act No. 92/2012 and Law Decree No. 148/2015 (as modified by Article. 1 paragraph 204, Act No. 234/2021), occupational provisions are compulsory for those employers, with at least one employee, who is not covered by the ordinary intervention of the short-time earning fund public scheme.

The constitution of the funds is delegated to the comparatively more representative trade union organizations at national level through collective agreements. The purpose of the funds is to provide workers with protection in cases of reduction or suspension of work, for the same reasons provided under the public CIG-CIGS scheme.

The occupational funds must guarantee an ordinary allowance at least equal to the public benefit, for the same duration. The benefits of the funds are subject to the cumulative duration limit of twenty-four months in a five-year period. The bilateral funds can also provide for other unemployment benefits.

173. The complexity of this system, especially for the almost coercive involvement of trade unions, seems to be perceived by the legislator, who provided, as a precautionary measure, for the alternative instrument of the Fund for Salary Integration (FIS). This fund, run by INPS, becomes compulsory for those employers with at least one employee, belonging to sectors, types and size classes that do not fall within the scope of application of public CIG and who have not constituted yet occupational funds. FIS guarantees, in relation to the same causes of the public scheme: to employers who, in the six months preceding the date of submission of the application, have employed, on average, up to five employees, the benefit for a maximum duration of thirteen weeks in a two-year period; to employers who, in the six months preceding the date of submission of the application, have employed on average more than five employees, the benefit for a maximum duration of twenty-six weeks in a two-year period . Workers are also paid family allowances. The FIS' benefits are subject to the cumulative duration limit of twenty-four months in a five-year period. The FIS does not provide other additional services. FIS benefits are only paid to those employees who have accrued at least ninety days of effective work in the productive unit for which the firm requires the intervention; this condition does not operate for the ordinary intervention due to transitory involuntary events which cannot be imputed to the employers or to the workers. FIS benefits are just suspended (not withdrawn) in case of recipients' work activities. FIS interventions are authorized by the INPS local offices.

174. The contribution to occupational CIG-CIGS and to the FIS, as established by ministerial decree, is entirely private and shared between employers and workers, in the measure of two-thirds and one-third; the contribution must guarantee the pre-constitution of adequate continuing resources, to be also verified on the basis of the budgets estimates. The firms who apply for the interventions are also requested to pay an additional contribution. From 2025, employers with up to five employees who have not requested FIS benefits for at least twenty-four months, are rewarded with the reduction of the additional contribution.

All the occupational funds, including FIS, are subject to the payment of the notional contribution for the purpose of pension's rights and amount.

The benefits provided by occupational funds and FIS have, however, a very heavy constraint, that of a balanced budget: benefits cannot be provided in the absence of available resources, that is interventions paid by all types of funds are conditioned to the establishment of specific financial reserves and within the limits of the resources already acquired. This, for bilateral solidarity funds and for FIS, implies that the administrator committee must also prepare, in addition to budget estimates at eight years, the changes of benefits and contributions necessary to guarantee the budget balance.

§5. ISCRO for the Self-Employed

175. The extraordinary allowance for income and operational continuity (ISCRO), established by the budget Act for 2021 (Act No. 178/2020), and largely inspired by a recent draft law of the CNEL, is targeted to the self-employed enrolled in the 'Fourth Fund' of the INPS (Article 2 paragraph 26, Act No. 335/1995). The benefit is a temporary measure, for the three-year period 2021–2023. Its goal is to preserve, in times of downturn, the professional activity of self-employed: a short-time earning fund, in substance. ISCRO is subject to the following requirements: (a) not to be holders of direct pension treatment and not to be insured with other compulsory social security scheme; (b) not be beneficiaries of citizenship income; (c) have produced an income from self-employment, in the year preceding the submission of the application, lower than 50% of the average income from self-employment achieved in the previous three years; (d) have declared, in the year preceding the submission of the application, an income not exceeding EUR 8,145.00 (revalued annually); (e) be in compliance with the compulsory social security contribution; (f) have a VAT number active for at least four years, on the date of submission of the application. The benefit paid is equal to 25%, on a six-monthly basis, of the last income certified by the Revenue Agency and is paid for six months; the amount of the allowance cannot in any case exceed the limit of EUR 800.00 per month and cannot be less than EUR 250.00 per month (revalued annually). The benefit is not taxed and does not involve crediting of notional contributions. A further limitation is that the benefit cannot be requested more than once in the three-year period. The disbursement of the allowance is accompanied by the participation of workers in professional training courses. ISCRO is financed by an increase in the contribution of workers enrolled in the 'Fourth Fund' of the INPS. As often, however, the payment of ISCRO is subject to the presence of the funds allocated for the purpose.

Part VIII. Pensions

Chapter 1. Pensions for Wage-Earners

§1. Old-Age Pension

I. Beneficiaries

176. Economic provision for the elderly is the object of obligatory invalidity, old-age, and survivors' insurance. The general system for employees is administered by INPS (National Social Welfare Institute).[95] The criterion of administration of resources used in the Italian pension system is that of distribution. In the distribution system the pension paid is financed by the contribution revenue from active workers.

The Italian pension system was reformed with Act No. 335 of 1995, which transformed the pension regime from a pay-based system to a contribution-based system, while the criterion for managing resources remained unchanged. The new regulations lay down a long period of transition and apply fully to workers who have been newly taken on at the moment when the reform entered into force. The long transition period provided for the coming into full effect of the reform has caused the co-existence within our pension system of two different regimes: the old pay-based system and the new contribution-based system. In particular, the new contributory system applies entirely to workers employed from 1 January 1996 onwards. The pay-based system, on the other hand, continues to apply *pro quota* only to workers who began their employment relationship before the 1 January 1996. For these workers a mixed system applies: in other words, the contribution system applies in relation to the proportion of pension accrued from 1 January 1996 onwards, and the pay-based system applies in relation to the proportion of pension accrued during the preceding years.

95. The main legal references of the obligatory pension system are the following: Act No. 153 of 1969; Act No. 297 of 1982; Act No. 421 of 1992; Law Decree No. 503 of 1992; Law Decree No. 373 of 1993; Act No. 537 of 1993; Act No. 724 of 1994; Act No. 335 of 1995; Law Decree No. 579 of 1995; Legislative Decree No. 564 of 1996; Law Decree No. 565 of 1996; Law Decree No. 180 of 1997; Law Decree No. 184 of 1997; Law Decree No. 314 of 1997; Act No. 449 of 1997; Act No. 243/2004; Act No. 247/2007; Act No. 214/2011.

II. Conditions in the Pay-Based System

177. To be able to accede to old-age pension payment, workers must have fulfilled the age and insurance requirements and have ended the employment relationship (with the exception of initiating a new one later).[96] Moreover, they have to apply appropriately to INPS.

Our system has tended towards a progressive raising of the pensionable age. This was necessary both by a need to adapt to the European average and by a need to readjust the system in its parameters of administration. The lengthening of the average lifespan has in fact caused an increase in the total yield of pensions, which our system could not deal with any longer on the economic level. The pensionable age presently required in the pay-based system is 67 years for women and men; the pensionable age, however, is automatically increased every two years in relation to the growth of the average life expectancy.[97]

Raising the pensionable age has also been encouraged by other measures. The objective of the legislator of Act No. 214/2011 is that of reaching the pensionable age of 70 years by 2050. In the meantime, the legislation favours agreements between employers and employees to carry on working until 70 years of age.[98]

Discontinuous workers, visually disabled and disabled greater than 80% have a lower pensionable age. Workers employed in what are generally considered hard and dangerous jobs or in harmful jobs, such as working with asbestos, and working mothers also enjoy a reduction in pensionable age.[99]

178. To be able to receive pension payment at least twenty years of obligatory insurance and contributions or the equivalent (notional, voluntary, or by redemption) are required.

The increase in the contribution requirement to twenty years, however, tends to vitiate against the insurance coverage of seasonal and occasional workers and those employed in a generally precarious way, as well as those who come into the job market late[100], or who are part of various regimes of provision.

Workers employed in hard and dangerous jobs, among others those involving asbestos, enjoy reductions in contribution years.[101]

---

96. Article 1, 7° comma, Law Decree No. 503 of 1992.
97. Articles 1, Law Decree No. 503 of 1992, and 11, Act No. 724 of 1994.
98. Article 24, para. 4, Act No. 214/2011.
99. Articles 1 and 2 of Law Decree No. 374 of 1993; Art. 1, para. 37, Act No. 335/1995; Art. 13, para. 8, Act No. 257/1992; Art. 47 Act No. 326/2033; Art. 1, paras 21–22, Act No. 247/2007; Art. 1, para. 115, Act No. 190/2014; Art. 1, para. 274, Act No. 208/2015; Law Decree No. 67/2011; Art. 1, paras 147 and 148, Act No. 205/2017; Art. 1, para. 4, Act No. 335/1995.
100. Indeed, for those who can claim an insurance seniority of at least 25 years and have been employed for at least ten years, even if not consecutive, for periods of less than 52 weeks in the calendar year, the legislator has provided a reduction of the contribution years required to 15.
101. Articles 1 and 2 of Law Decree No. 374 of 1993; Art. 1, para. 37, Act No. 335/1995; Art. 13, para. 8, Act No. 257/1992; Art. 47 Act No. 326/2033; Art. 1, paras 21–22, Act No. 247/2007; Art. 1, para. 115, Act No. 190/2014; Art. 1, para. 274, Act No. 208/2015; Law Decree No. 67/2011; Art. 1, paras 147 and 148, Act No. 205/2017; Art. 1, para. 4, Act No. 335/1995. *See also* the Constitutional Court decisions No. 434/2002 and No. 369/2003.

III. Conditions in the Contribution System

179. The requirements for access to pensions in the contribution system are the following:

- reaching the pensionable age of 67 years, for men and women, destined to automatically increase every two years in relation to the growth of the average life expectancy, or alternatively 42 years and 10 months, for men, and 41 years and 10 months for women, of contributions;
- minimum period of contribution of twenty years;
- the total of contributions paid must be such that the total of the pension corresponding to them is at least equal to 1.5 times the state social allowance, or alternatively the worker must be at least 71 years of age (in this case the minimum contribution period is five years).

Another hypothesis of retirement under the contribution system is the following:

- 64 years of age, destined to automatically increase every two years in relation to the growth of the average life expectancy;
- minimum period of contribution of twenty years;
- the total of contributions paid must be such that the total of the pension corresponding to them is at least equal to 2.8 times the state social allowance.

Again, Article. 1 paragraph 87 of Act No. 234/2021 introduced, for the year 2022, the so-called quota 102: according to this, a worker can retire if has at least 64 years of age and a minimum contribution period of thirty-eight years.

For retirements on the basis of the amount of contributions and independently of age, the legislation provides for a 'window' of three months, for private employees, and of six months, for public employees: that is, the retirement of the worker who has fulfilled the scheme requirements is delayed of three or six months, accordingly.

Finally, Act No. 26/2019 (as modified by Article. 1 paragraph 94, Act No. 234/2021) provided the so-called women option: women with 58 years of age, if employed, or with 59 years of age if self-employed can retire if they have accrued thirty-five years of contributions within 31 December 2021, on condition that they opt for the pension calculation entirely under the contribution system (rather than the pro quota mixed system calculation). In this case a complex system of 'window' that delays the effective retirement of twelve to eighteen months is however applied.

180. Thus, pensionable age is now fixed at 67 years for both men and women, however destined to automatically increase every two years in relation to the growth of the average life expectancy. With each year of increase in age, larger coefficients of transformation are granted; coefficients of transformation are the multiplier of the individual contribution total and are linked to life expectancy and age of retirement.[102]

Reductions in the age of taking a pension are permitted in cases of discontinuous workers, visually disabled and disabled greater than 80% have a lower pensionable age. Workers employed in what are generally considered hard and dangerous jobs or in harmful jobs, such as working with asbestos and working mothers also enjoy a reduction in pensionable age.[103]

The objective of the legislator of Act No. 214/2011 is that of reaching the pensionable age of 70 years by 2050. In the meantime, the legislation favours agreements between employers and employees to carry on working until 70 years of age.[104]

181. Pension reform of 1995 eliminated the institution of supplementation of pensions up to the minimum. In the new system, however, the role of supplementation to the minimum has been entrusted to the state social allowance. Whenever the pension is lower than the income limits, the worker falls back into the area of coverage by the social allowance.

IV. Pension Calculation in the Pay-Based System

182. The old-age pension is a welfare benefit based on the age of the individual. According to the pay-based system, the total of the pension is determined by calculating the average of the salaries received in a certain period of reference. More precisely, the calculation of the old-age pension is the following:

> pensionable income (average of taxable pay received in a determined period of reference)
>
> ×
>
> a quota or rate of yield of 2% for each year of contribution accredited (years of contributions), within the maximum limit of forty years of contributions.
>
> =
>
> the maximum pension will be equal to 80% (forty years × 2%) of the average pay in the period of reference.

183. The period of reference for the calculation of pensionable pay is equal to:

---

102. *See* below sub-para. V of this section.
103. Articles 1 and 2 of Law Decree No. 374 of 1993; Art. 1, para. 37, Act No. 335/1995; Art. 13, para. 8, Act No. 257/1992; Art. 47 Act No. 326/2033; Art. 1, paras 21–22, Act No. 247/2007; Art. 1, para. 115, Act No. 190/2014; Art. 1, para. 274, Act No. 208/2015; Law Decree No. 67/2011; Art. 1, paras 147 and 148, Act No. 205/2017; Art. 1, para. 4, Act No. 335/1995.
104. Article 24, para. 4, Act No. 214/2011.

- the whole working life for workers employed from 1 January 1993 onwards; this except for the possibility of cancelling out the worst years from the calculation, up to a maximum limit of 25% of the total of years covered by contribution;[105]
- the last ten years of contributions, for workers who on 31 December 1992 could present a period of contribution equal to or greater than fifteen years;[106]
- the last five years of contributions, increased with the contribution periods that exist between 31 December 1992 and the date immediately preceding that of the start of the pension, for workers who had less than fifteen years of contributions on 31 December 1992.[107]

184. It must be considered that by now two notions of taxable pay exist, which are valid both for the purposes of determining the pension and for defining the contribution to be paid.[108] The first, established by Article 12 of Act No. 153 of 1969,[109] consists of 'all that which the worker receives from the employer in money or in kind, gross of any deduction, in dependence of the employee-employer relationship', this except for certain items explicitly indicated. In particular the following are excluded: refund of expenses; cash and years of service allowances, payments as gifts, daily allowances, and fixed-sum travel expenses; sums paid on occasion of the termination of a working relationship to encourage early retirement; emoluments for family allowances, in cases permitted by law, paid directly by the employer; allowances for employees abroad; emoluments for canteen services and transport offered by the employer and their relative substitute payments; expenses for study grants, for kindergartens, and for company clubs and associations. This definition of pay has been modified by Law Decree No. 314 of 1997, which established the parity of taxable income for pension purposes with that of the taxable amount for fiscal purposes. In particular, what is considered taxable income from work as an employee for pension purposes is that 'which is constituted by all sums and values in general, received for whatever reason in the tax period, even under the form of free payments, in relation to the employee-employer relationship'. The definition of taxable pay laid down by Article 12 will be valid for incomes accruing prior to January 1998, given the coming into effect of Law Decree No. 314 of 1997; the new notion, on the other hand, will have effect for incomes accruing after that date. Last, it must be remembered that certain legal provisions have established the partial exclusion from contribution of 'payments set out in collective company contracts, or rather in second-level collective agreements, the payment or totals of which are uncertain, and the structure of which is correlated by the same collective contract to measurement of increases in productivity, quality and other elements of competitiveness taken as indicators of the economic progress of the company and of its results' (the so-called de-contribution regime).[110]

---

105. Article 1, Law Decree No. 373 of 1993.
106. Article 1, 17° comma Act No. 335 of 1993.
107. Article 3, para. 1, Law Decree No. 503/1992.
108. *See* more specifically Part II of this study.
109. *See also* Art. 17 of Law Decree No. 503 of 1992; Art. 2, XV and XVIII comma, Act No. 335 of 1995.
110. Article 1, Act No. 608 of 1996; Act No. 153 of 1997.

185. The total amount of pensions is periodically adjusted to the cost of living. The adjustment mechanism, known as automatic equalization, occurs annually and has effect from 1 November every year. The percentage of variation is calculated on the average value of the ISTAT index of consumer prices for worker and employee families. The adjustment mechanism has been periodically revised downwards either by increasing the period between the adjustments, or by applying it according to ranges of pension amounts, or finally by temporarily suspending its operativity.[111]

In addition to pension payments, pensioners benefit, where conditions exist, from the family income support.[112]

186. A pension ceiling operates only for the purposes of determining the size of pensions: indeed, a maximum ceiling for the annual pensionable pay exists; the pay within this maximum ceiling is taken into account according to the ordinary yield rate of 2%. Pay exceeding the ceiling is taken into account by groups according to yield rates that decrease progressively.[113] On the other hand, the entire taxable pay remains subject to contribution.

The contributory minimum, or in other words, the threshold below which contribution may not fall, is equal to 9.5% of the minimum monthly pension of the affected year.[114]

Article 1 of Act No. 389 of 1989 establishes, last, that the pay to be taken as the basis of calculation of contributions cannot be lower than the total of payments established by laws, regulations, and collective contracts stipulated by the unions that are most representative on a national level; or than the total of payments established by collective or individual agreements, whenever there derives a total of payment that is higher than that laid down by the collective contract (in the case of the existence of a variety of contracts for the same category, the one stipulated by the comparatively most representative union organizations is taken into account).[115]

A supplementation of pension to the minimum guarantees the sufficiency at the lower end of old-age pension payments, to prevent the sums of pensions from being laughable. It is paid if the insurance and contribution minimums have nevertheless been achieved.

However, it is to be remembered that the supplement to the minimum was abolished by Article 1, comma XVI of Act No. 335 of 1995 for all workers beginning employment after 1 January 1996 (and possibly for those who, even though they

111. Article 11, Legislative Decree No. 503 of 1992; Art. 1, 33° comma, Act No. 335 of 1995; Art. 14, Act No. 724 of 1994; Art. 69, Act No. 388/2000. *See also* Art. 1, para. 19, Act No. 247/2007; Art. 1, para. 236, Act No. 228/2012.
112. *See*, for more details, Part IV of this study.
113. Article 21, Act No. 67 of 1998; Art. 12, Legislative Decree No. 503 of 1998; Art. 59, 1° comma, Act No. 449 of 1997.
114. A particular criterion for determining the minimum level is laid down for part-time employment (Art. 1, 4° comma, Act No. 389 of 1989), for agricultural waged work (Legislative Decree No. 146 of 1997) and for work in building (Art. 29, Act No. 341 of 1995).
115. *See also* Art. 2, 25° comma, Act No. 549 of 1995. The rule of the minimum level has, however, certain exceptions: such is the regulation of pay for availability in temporary work contracts (Art. 9, Act No. 196 of 1997) and the regulations regarding collective contracts of realignment (Art. 5, Act No. 608 of 1990; Art. 23, Act No. 196 of 1997).

have the right to the mixed system, opt for the contribution system). In the new system, the role of supplementation to the minimum should be affected by the social allowance payment.

Finally, the legislation concerning income aggregation has had, over time, an important and tumultuous development. At present, however, old-age pensions can be entirely combined with any kind of income from work.[116] This trend is justified by the necessity to avoid or disclose pensioners' 'black' work; therefore, the principle of solidarity, which justified at the origins a partial income aggregation, has progressively been overtaken.

V. Pension Calculation in the Contribution System

187. Act No. 335 of 1995 has radically modified the whole pension arrangement. It introduced, in particular, the contribution system of calculation of pensions. Calculation of benefit has as its first parameter contributions paid: this calculation consists in multiplying the total of contributions accredited to the worker over his/her whole life, or rather the individual contribution total, by a coefficient which is established by law. This coefficient varies according to the retirement age of the worker and has been determined by taking into account demographic trends, life expectancy and GDP. The coefficient is re-determined every two years by a Ministerial Decree. The criterion for management of the resources remains that of distribution. The individual contribution total is an accounting fiction valid for the purposes of pension calculation; that is to say, the actual accumulated funds reserved for the insured individual do not correspond to it: pensions are in substance paid by the contributions paid in by those who are working. Although, the rate of annual provision from taxable remuneration for the calculation of the pension now coincides with the actual contribution levied. In addition, some safeguard clauses in the system are laid down, as we shall see: contribution and levy quotas and transformation coefficients may, indeed, be varied where the capacity of the system requires. The new contribution system is applied in full to workers taken on after 1 January 1996.

188. Let us look in detail at the mechanism of pension calculation:

individual contribution total (sum of all contribution years accredited to the interested party, re-valued annually on the basis of the average variation of gross domestic product in the previous five years)

×

transformation coefficients (representative of the average remaining life expectancy, calculated on the basis of statistical-actuarial criteria, in connection with the age of retirement)

=

116. Act No. 133/2008.

gross annual pension, which is re-evaluated annually on the basis of inflation (automatic equalization).

The rate of annual provision, or, in other words, the calculation rate is fixed, for employees, at 33% of taxable income. The contribution total is subject to an annual contribution and pensionable maximum, which may be annually re-evaluated. More favourable coefficients of transformation are laid down for workers in hard, dangerous jobs or in harmful jobs, visually disabled and mothers. In both cases the mechanism is alternative to the possibility of gaining the pension at a lower age than normal. The calculation rate, like the contribution quotas and thus the relationship between them, or in other words the yield of the contributions paid in, may be periodically modified depending on variations in GDP and in the relation of contributions to pensions, by means of an administrative act. The coefficients of transformation may also be altered by administrative act where variations in GDP or in the relationship between contributions and pensions consequent to variations in the average duration of life or in demographic factors justify the change.

189. As regards taxable income, the same rules apply as those described in relation to the pay-based system. Let us briefly remember here that for incomes accrued before January 1998, taxable income is considered to be 'all that the employee receives in money or in kind, gross of any deduction, in dependence of the employment relationship', while for incomes accrued after that date, taxable income for welfare purposes coincides with that taxable from a fiscal point of view and consists of 'all the sums and values in general, for whatever reason received in the tax period, even in the form of free payments, in relation to the employment relationship'.

190. The mechanism of automatic equalization is the same as that already described for the pay-based system of pension calculation. More specifically, the mechanism for adjustment has an annual incidence and takes effect from 1 November every year. The percentage of variation is calculated on the basis of the average value of the ISTAT retail price index for workers' and white-collar employees' families.

In addition to the pension payment, pensioners may, where the correct conditions apply, benefit from the family allowance.[117]

As in the pay-based regime, the discipline of aggregation allows the worker to totally combine old-age pension and income from dependent work or self-employment.

§2. Survivors Pension

191. Death figures as one of the events covered by the obligatory invalidity, old-age, and survivors' insurance. In Italy's welfare system a distinction is made between the convertible pension and the indirect pension.

117. *See*, for more details, Part IV of this study.

The convertible pension is that paid to the survivors of a worker who at the moment of death had already retired; the following are convertible: old-age pensions, invalidity pensions, disability pensions, years-of-service pensions. The following are not convertible: the invalidity allowance, the social allowance, and the yields of insurance against injury at work.

The indirect pension, on the other hand, gains title from the death of the worker, who must have accrued the insurance and contribution requirements laid down by the law for the relevant payments, that is for old-age and invalidity pensions. When the worker has not qualified for the indirect pension and his/her death was not caused by industrial accident, the survivors' relatives are entitled to a lump-sum payment, on condition that they have fulfilled the income requirements for the social allowance.

192. The following have the right to the survivors' pension: the spouse, included the partner in civil unions, and children, including those recognized as having equal rights; in the absence of spouse or partner and children, the parents; in the absence of these also, unmarried brothers and sisters.

The requirements for entitlement to payment are the following:

- the benefit applies to the spouse, independent of any objective cause; the right is cancelled if the spouse remarries, with the possible re-settlement of the quota due to the children;
- children and others recognized as equal (including posthumous children married at the date of death) have a right to the benefit if, at the moment of death, they were, in addition to being dependent on the person giving title to the pension, less than 18 years old; students of middle and professional schools between 18 and 21 years of age; university students between 18 and 26 years of age; disabled persons of any age;
- the parents (here including adoptive, caring and foster parents) may benefit from the pension if they are older than 65 years of age, disabled, not in receipt of another pension;
- brothers and sisters unmarried have a right to the pension if they are disabled, are not entitled to another pension (marriage after obtaining the pension is a cause of the elimination of the right).

Grandchildren dependents from the deceased worker are equalled to children; the existence in life of the parents of the minors of age does not represent an obstacle, when it is proved that they are unable to provide to the children.[118]

In the case of divorce, the divorced spouse has the right to the pension on condition that he/she has not remarried, is in receipt of a divorce allowance, and that the relationship from which the pension draws origin is antecedent to the divorce. If after the divorce the defunct person remarries, the judge will have to define the quotas of pension to be paid to the first and the second spouse, in relation, among others, to the length of the cohabitation.[119]

118. *See* Constitutional Court No. 180/1999.
119. *See* Constitutional Court No. 419/1999.

The pension is also due to the spouse who is legally separated; if, however, the spouse had a culpable responsibility in the separation, he/she will have the right to the pension only if he/she turns out to be already in receipt of alimony payments from the defunct individual.

The survivor sentenced with a final judgment of the murder of the deceased worker is not entitled to a pension.

193. Individuals who are entitled receive the pension according to particular criteria of comparison between them:

- the spouse has the right to 60% of the pension of the defunct person;
- the children have the right to 20% or 40% each, depending on whether there is also a spouse present; the only child without parents has the right to 70%; the grandchildren are equalled to children;
- brothers, sisters, or parents have the right to 15% each.

In any case the total size of the pension may neither be lower than 60% nor higher than 100% of the direct pension.

In the presence of only one survivor having title, pensions benefit from supplementation to the minimum according to the usual criteria. In the case of the presence of more than one pension (either direct or convertible), the benefit is granted on only one payment.

Pensions have limits of aggregation with the income of the beneficiary: pensions may be combined with beneficiaries' income on the basis of coefficients of reduction of pension payments (25%, 40%, and 50%) in function with three distinct income thresholds, related to three, four, and five times the minimum payment of general obligatory social insurance; such limits do not apply when children who are of minor age, students or handicapped are present.

194. The survivors' pension follows in the contribution system the same rules laid down in the pay-based system, with the exception that the requirements and mechanisms of calculation will naturally be those of the contributory system. Obviously, it is applied the coefficient of transformation of 57 years of age even when death occurs at a lower age.

It should be underlined here how the abolition of supplementation of pensions to the minimum and its substitution with the social allowance operated by the new system renders the regulation of pensions that do not reach the minimum level problematic, provided that social allowance has a non-reversible character.

Chapter 2. Pensions for the Self-Employed

§1. Pension Provision for Small Business

195. Within the INPS there are three special funds that guarantee insurance coverage for invalidity, old age, and for surviving dependents for certain categories of self-employed workers:

(1) the special fund for direct cultivators of the land, sharecroppers and tenant farmers;
(2) the special fund for craft workers;
(3) the special fund for those involved in commercial activities.

These funds, which have been created into the general INPS system, are regulated by Act No. 233 of 1990, even if they are special schemes. This law radically reformed the previous regulations both in relation to the financing criteria of the funds and to the payments given out. For the self-employed registered for the first time in the obligatory social insurance system after 1 January 1996, payment of pension will take place, instead, with the system introduced by the pension reform of Act No. 335 of 1995.

196. The Act of 1990 introduced the system of retributive calculation of pensions for small businessmen and women. Contributions and payments are made proportional to the income of the company reported in the previous tax year for the purposes of personal income tax (IRPEF). Contributions are owed within the minimum and maximum limits of income; on totals of income exceeding the annual minimum and up to the maximum limit of taxable income higher rates are owed. The contributions and payments of direct cultivators of the land, sharecroppers and tenant farmers are, in contrast, proportional to the conventional average income that is determined annually by the Department of Employment. The payment system lays down that the calculation of pensions is carried out by making reference to the average income of the last ten years of contributions (or of a lower number of years prior to the start date of the pension if the insured person has not reached ten years of contributions); a quota equal to 2% of company income corresponds to every year of contribution, up to a maximum pensionable ceiling; the maximum pension is equal to 80% of income, with forty years of contributions. For the purposes of calculation of a pension the company income is re-evaluated every year. Furthermore, the pension is subject to annual revision. The pension age is fixed at 67 years.

197. The 1995 reform generalized the contribution system of calculation of pensions. We already had the opportunity to describe that above.[120] When the reform is fully in operation, there will be a virtually total recognition of the equal values of self-employed workers and employees in pension calculation. For the self-employed, however, some differences will remain. The rate for pension calculation,

120. *See* Ch. 1 of this part.

in particular, is fixed at 24% of taxable pay for the self-employed, instead of 33% for employees.[121] In addition, attainment of the right to an old-age pension is not subject to the cessation of working activities, in contrast to the situation for employees.

§2. Pension Provision for Freelance Professionals

198. For various categories of the self-employed, the so-called freelance professionals, there are obligatory forms of social insurance coverage managed by autonomous funds or organizations, which are now private bodies. The main professional funds are those of: lawyers; chartered accountants; surveyors; engineers and architects; notaries; accountants; consultants (ENPACL); doctors and dentists (ENPAM); pharmacists (ENPAF); veterinary surgeons (ENPAV); biologists (ENPAB) and industrial experts (EPPI). The insurance covers those professionals who are officially registered with their professional association and are actually engaged in work. Contributions are proportional to a percentage of the professional income declared for IRPEF purposes; generally, the average of fifteen years of professional income, chosen from the best years out of a longer period, is taken into consideration, depending on the system involved.[122] The payments consist of old-age, invalidity, and surviving dependents' pensions, paid out according to regulations that vary from one fund to another. The Pension Reform Act No. 335 of 1995 set out provisions aimed at harmonizing, with respect to the autonomy of the Funds, the regulations of the various pension systems with the general principles that constitute the new pension system. In particular, Article 3 of the Act lays down the linking of the basis of pension calculation to that for the self-employed: or rather, the income relative to a period of fifteen years is to be taken into consideration. The reform, in addition, sanctions the possibility for individual funds to opt for the adoption of the contribution system for the calculation of pensions. Cessation of subscription to a particular pension fund before accruing the years of service necessary for a pension gives the right to restitution of the contributions already paid. The worker has, however, the possibility of accumulating the various periods of contributions made under various funds. Finally, these private funds are called to guarantee their financial equilibrium.

§3. Pension Coverage of Self-Employed Workers Registered with the 'Fourth Fund' of the INPS

199. The Pension Reform Act No. 335 of 1995 established a particular regulation, as a final addition to the pension system, for those self-employed workers without welfare coverage until then. Indeed, the regulation applies to workers having a co-ordinate and continuative relationship with a particular company or institution

121. In this regard *see* Ch. 2 of this part.

122. In some cases the contributions are supplemented by sums to be paid by the clients through the invoice.

(the so-called para-employees), to individuals who do self-employed work as their regular profession, and to freelance professionals without registration with a professional association. Since 1 January 1996 these individuals have been required to subscribe to a specific fund within the INPS, which is intended to supply pension coverage for invalidity, old age, and dependants. The pensions are calculated with the contribution system. At present the total contribution rate, paid one-third by the worker and two-thirds by the contracting company or institution, is 33% of the income from professional activity reported for income tax purposes (IRPEF), for those who are not included in other compulsory schemes; for workers who are already included in other compulsory pension schemes, the contribution rate is lowered to 24%. Contributions are subject to maximum and minimum income limits. With respect to the minimum contribution limit, workers will have the right to the full contribution accreditation only on the condition that they have paid in a contribution not less than that calculated on the minimum income limit established for self-employed workers registered with the special funds of the INPS; if the contribution paid in does not reach the above-mentioned level, the pension months to be accredited are reduced proportionally.

Chapter 3. Supplementary Social Security

§1. Field of Application

200. After years of interminable debate and countless proposals, Law Decree No. 124 of 1993 established the regulations for private pension funds.[123] The law defines private pension funds as 'those forms of welfare for the payment of pensions which are complementary to the obligatory public system, with the aim of ensuring higher levels of welfare cover'. The regulations originally established were then integrated and profoundly modified by later provisions, such as Law Decree No. 585 of 1993 and the Pension Reform Act No. 335 of 1995. Then, Law Decree No. 47 of 2000 laid down favourable fiscal treatments for all the quotas of income used for pension purposes. Finally, Law Decree No. 252/2005 completely reformed the discipline. The introduction of regulation of private funds responds to the need, which has been noticed more and more in our country, to entrust the realization of social policies not exclusively to public bodies but more and more often to collective organizations, if not even to private operators. In particular, on the occasion of the pension reforms of the 1990s, the legislator intended to make private complementary provision, instituted by collective bodies, a second pillar of our pension system, next to that of basic public welfare. A third pillar has been identified in the form of individual pension. At the bottom of these political choices can clearly be seen the progressive crisis in public finances and the consequent social welfare deficit of the public social security system. This choice, which is clear under the political point of view, has not been supported by a clear-cut legislation and has caused criticisms.

Private pension cover is managed according to the criteria of capitalization and has an optional character. It requires the use of additional financial resources compared to those destined for the basic welfare system: these resources are obviously only at the disposal of workers of the stronger productive categories. The complementary pension systems are burdened, as we shall see, with a 'solidarity contribution' for the benefit of the public welfare system.

201. Prior to this organic systemization of the phenomenon, forms of supplementary provision had come into existence in various productive sectors in the absence of a legal point of reference. The legislator laid down a gradual extension of the new regulations to pre-existing funds as well. The preservation of the previously applicable regulations for contributions and payments was guaranteed to individuals registered with the said funds; however, if the fund reveals financial imbalances, the old regulations remain in force only for those who, on the date the new regulations came into force, had already accrued the requirements laid down by the institutional documents of the funds for pension payment. The legislator, in addition, subordinated payment of the complementary pension to the maturing of the obligatory pension payment.

123. Law Decree No. 124 of 1993 carries out the delegation of Art. 3, para. 1V, Act No. 421 of 1992.

202. The legislator also regulated certain aspects of individual private pensions, which are realized either by means of adhesion to pension funds or by means of insurance contracts. In particular the right to pay contributions to the benefit of dependent family members instead of to one's own benefit is recognized. In addition, a system of tax exemption of contributions paid in applies to individual pension funds, as is also the case for complementary pension funds. From this point of view the decision to encourage pension saving over other types of saving is clear, even if it is realized in an individual form.

203. The forms of complementary pension provision are available to all workers, as long as they are contributors to a basic obligatory pension regime. Membership is voluntary. Thus, besides employees in the public and private sectors, the self-employed, freelance professionals, the 'para-employed' (i.e., workers who offer their services to a company in a continuous and coordinated manner), and members of cooperatives can also avail themselves of supplementary cover. Employees, as shall be made clear below, may only subscribe to funds with fixed contributions.

§2. Benefits

204. Pension funds are collective welfare provision funds that operate on the basis of the principle of capitalization, or rather according to criteria of the amount due. This means that the amounts of pension payments and contributions must guarantee the financial and accounting balance of the fund. Funds may be with defined contributions or with defined payment. Funds with defined contributions are those in which the total amount of the pension is not predetermined, but depends on the results of the management of the resources set aside by means of periodical contributions; contributions to these funds are, on the other hand, predetermined. This type of fund is the same as that applicable to employees. Funds with defined payment are, in contrast, those where the intended result is established a priori, that is to say, the total pension payment: for this pre-arranged total the contribution is periodically adjusted on the basis of variations in the general economic situation and in the profits of the investments of capital made by the fund. Self-employed workers can choose either the fund with defined payment or that with defined contribution. The choice of funds with defined payment is not permitted to employed workers precisely because of the variability of the contribution payments, which does not fit well with the receipt of a generally fixed income.

205. Another important distinction is that between closed and open funds. Funds constituted on a company basis or on the basis of a certain category of worker or profession are known as closed funds. Open funds are those set up by companies that professionally operate in the financial sector. Originally, the worker, who is free to subscribe to a pension fund or not, was limited, though, to the company, category, or professional community he/she belonged to; he/she could, therefore, only join funds constituted in the area of his/her company or profession. Now, the discipline changed and the worker is free to subscribe to an open pension fund.

Closed funds may be instituted by: contracts and collective agreements; agreements between self-employed or freelance workers; regulations of authorities or companies; agreements between working members in work and production cooperatives. Open funds are created on the initiative of financial intermediaries which must be recognized by law, that is to say, banks, estate agents, insurance companies, and companies managing joint investment funds. The statutes and regulations of funds must establish the formal procedures for membership of the fund, its characteristics, and its regulations. Funds can be constituted only in the form of an unrecognized association (Article 36 of the Civil Code) or 'legal person'. Constitution of funds in the form of internal company property is explicitly forbidden; this in order to avoid the scenario that a possible financial collapse of the employing company affects the fund. Workers' and employers' representatives participate equally in the organs of administration of the fund.

206. Complementary forms of pension provision can regard the same events that are covered by public welfare regimes: old age, invalidity, disability, death, illness, industrial accidents, and professional diseases. However, at present, the main area of activity of this form of provision is pension coverage for old age. The requirements for access to pension payment are established by the constitutive documents of the funds, according to the above-mentioned amount-due criteria belonging to the capitalization system. However, the law lays down certain limits. In the first place, a complementary old-age pension is only allowed on attainment of the pensionable age established in the obligatory system that the individual belongs to; the minimum insurance period is fixed at five years. Pensions can be paid as a lump sum for the 50% of the final contribution total and for the other 50% as annuity; small annuities can be paid as lump sum.

In cases of cessation of the enterprise, which causes the employees' inoccupation for a period longer than forty-eight months, the worker can ask the complementary pension five years earlier than in the obligatory system. Moreover, unemployed for more than twenty-four months can ask the complementary pension ten years earlier than in the obligatory system. Workers can also ask for an integrative temporary pension corresponding to the contribution total accrued within a fund with defined contributions (so-called RITA) five years earlier than in the obligatory system, provided that they have accrued in the obligatory system at least twenty years contributions; RITA will be substituted by the normal integrative pension once reached the pensionable age provided.

Finally, it is also possible to ask for an anticipation in capital of the pension matured. Anticipated payments can be permitted, among others, for health expenses and, after eight years of subscription to the fund, for purchase of a home, or other necessities of the pensioner.

207. When the conditions of subscription to the form of complementary pension are no longer fulfilled, the worker may opt for transfer to another fund or for the redemption of his/her own contributions. The power of transfer of one's own individual position to another fund or to individual forms of pension exists after two years of subscription to a fund; the above-mentioned insurance condition is set aside when access to the new fund matures in relation to the type of working activity done. In some cases, transfer from one fund to the other, with the preservation of the individual's position regarding contributions, and the transfer of the related capital cover, is operated directly by the law.

Redemption, on the other hand, is nothing other than recovering one's own contribution, including that paid in by the employer, increased according to the technical rate of profit of the fund, which can be asked when the conditions of subscription to the form of complementary pension are no longer fulfilled, In case of death, the pension status of the worker or the contribution total may be redeemed by the spouse, by the children or, if living as dependents, by the parents and by the heir nominated by the worker; in the absence of these individuals, the pension status is acquired by the fund. A partial redemption of 50% of the contribution total accrued can also be asked in cases of cessation of the enterprise, which causes the employees' inoccupation for a period not shorter than twelve months and not longer than forty-eight months and in case of CIG-CIGS.

§3. Financing

208. Management of financial resources is entrusted to specialized bodies, such as estate agents, companies managing joint investment funds; funds can opt for the establishment of agreements with insurance companies for the purpose of paying out pensions. The financial resources of the funds must be deposited with a bank that is distinct from the manager of the fund, to prevent their improper use; this bank is obliged to carry out the instructions of the manager, providing these are not contrary to the law, to the statutes of the fund, and to the investment criteria defined by the relevant Ministerial Decree.

209. The management of pension funds is subject to the authorization of the Pension Fund Supervisory Committee (COVIP) at the Ministry of Labour. The COVIP is also expected to supervise the correct operation of the funds. The statutes and regulations of pension funds must be compatible with provisions published by the Committee. The COVIP enjoys wide regulatory power over establishment of: the procedures for presentation of applications for authorization; documents to accompany the application; the conditions for the issue of authorization.

210. Financing of funds falls to the named beneficiary and to the employer, or to the commissioning company or institution in the case of the self-employed or 'para-employed'. The contribution of the employee is established by the instituting documents of the funds, as a percentage of the basic pay for the calculation of the severance allowance; the contribution can also depend on particular elements of the wage or be identified by means of complete payment to the fund of some of these pay elements. The pension fund may, in addition, be financed with payment to it of a proportion of the annual sum set aside for the severance allowance. For workers employed after 28 April 1993, the date when the law on pension funds came into effect, it is laid down that the severance allowance might be completely directed towards the financing of the fund; the two parties in the working relationship may then be asked to add a further contribution. It is opportune here to make it clear that the severance allowance is a form of deferred payment for the worker, and a source of resources to invest for the company: every year a quota equal to the annual salary divided for 13.5 is set aside and only at the end of the working relationship is the total sum of these annual set-aside sums paid to the worker, even if, for specific reasons laid down by the law, anticipated payments of the severance allowance can be permitted before termination of the working relationship.[124] Investment of severance allowance in pension funds ought to guarantee workers an increased return on that quota of salary that is deferred. The pension funds into which the severance allowance is paid may also permit, in cases laid down by law, anticipated payments of the pension owing to the beneficiary.[125] In order to favour the expansion of supplementary schemes, Legislative Decree No. 252/2005 provided that the worker, within six months from the date of employment, must explicitly declare the intention of not investing the severance payment in occupational schemes; if the worker does not make this declaration, then the severance payment is automatically paid by the employer into a complementary pension scheme.[126] For the self-employed, freelance professionals, and working partners, contribution to pension funds is fixed as a percentage, respectively, of income declared for income tax purposes (IRPEF) and of taxable income taken into consideration for obligatory pension contributions.

211. Measures of tax relief are directed at lessening the extent of the burden of contribution for pension funds.

Contribution to funds is not subject to taxation: income set aside for pension purposes will be taxed at the moment of receipt in the form of a pension. However, financial profits deriving from investments made by pension funds are taxed; the total of the later pension payment is then exempted from tax up to a figure corresponding to the amount taken as taxation of the financial profits.

212. Sums paid for the payment of welfare provision are excluded from the taxable base for obligatory welfare contributions. This regulation is in consequence of a pronouncement of the Constitutional Court, which declared imposition of contributions on sums in their turn paid as contributions for complementary pension provision as illegitimate. The Court made it clear, in addition, that a total exemption of such sums from contribution to public welfare would be contrary to the principle of solidarity; this is especially true insomuch as contributions in the form of complementary provision are made up of medium-high incomes.[127] Thus, the law instituted a 'solidarity contribution' to be paid on sums destined for financing private complementary pensions, which is the responsibility exclusively of employers, to

124. In small companies with no more than twenty-five employees it is possible to make a partial payment of the retirement allowance to pension funds. This measure is aimed at helping small businesses, by preserving for them a quota of resources for investment.
125. Anticipated payments can be permitted after eight years of subscription to the fund, for health expenses, for purchase of a first home for the beneficiary or his/her child, or for maintenance or rebuilding work to the first home. Anticipated payments are allowed also during the parental leave (Art. 5, Legislative Decree No. 151/2001).
126. *See* Act No. 296/2006.
127. Constitutional Court, 3 Oct. 1990, No. 427.

the tune of 10%, for the benefit of the obligatory pension funds in which workers affected by the particular form of complementary pension are registered.[128] The solidarity contribution has been cut down and sometimes reduced to zero in certain sectors of the economy, such as publishing, with the intention of further encouraging complementary pension provision. In addition, quotas of profit-related pay earmarked to finance supplementary welfare provision are exempted from the solidarity contribution; profit-related pay is that linked to the productivity of the worker and the company.

128. A proportion of this contribution is to go to the guarantee fund instituted within INPS to protect against the risk of non-fulfilment on the part of employers of contribution obligations for complementary pension schemes.

Part IX. Handicapped Persons

Chapter 1. Beneficiaries

213. Civil invalidity benefits are a universal form of assistance for all the citizens based on the first paragraph of Article 38 of the Constitution. They are intended for those whose mental or physical health has been impaired and either never worked or have not been able to pay in the minimum amount of national insurance contributions to warrant a pension. The right to these benefits does not depend on any minimum requisites, and as such it has extremely tight earnings limits. The term 'civil invalid' is used to describe: citizens affected by inherited or acquired defects, even if they are progressive; those with mental impairments of an organic or metabolic nature; people with mental defects caused by sensory or functional problems. For these people to be covered by the benefit, they must have suffered a permanent reduction in their working capacity of no less than 74% or, if they are less than 18 years of age, must show persistent difficulty in carrying out the duties and functions of others of the same age.[129]

129. *See* Act No. 118 of 1971; Art. 9 of Law Decree No. 509 of 1988; Act No. 381 of 1970.

Chapter 2. Conditions

214. The first requirement for the right to civil invalidity benefits is Italian citizenship and residence. EU nationals and extra-communitarian people with residence permit, who reside in Italy for work purposes may also be eligible. Another condition is that earnings must be less than a periodically revaluated limit. The limit is divided according to the category and degree of invalidity. On reaching 67 years of age, the civil invalidity pension and allowance are automatically converted into the social allowance.

215. Payment and any re-calculation of this benefit take place in two stages: first a medical check, and then a procedural one. The medical check is carried out by special medical commission at the local health units. INPS is in charge of the administrative controls. The actual payment is also made by INPS, which can draw on a special fund for this purpose.

Chapter 3. Benefits

216. Benefits payable to civil invalids may be of three types:

- to the mutilated and civil invalids of over 18 years who are completely unable to work, the inability pension is paid: this is the case even where they are patients in an institute or rest home;[130]
- to the mutilated and civil invalids aged between 18 and 67 who cannot work and who have a reduction in their working capacity of not less than 74%, the invalidity allowance is paid;[131]
- to those below 18 years of age who face persistent difficulties in carrying out the duties and functions common to others of the same age, or who have hearing difficulties above a certain level and are receiving rehabilitation or medical treatment, or who frequent schools or training centres, the attendance allowance is paid.[132]

At present, the monthly amount for the three types of benefit is quite low. This basic level can however be increased, depending on the claimant's age and earnings. The benefits cannot be paid if the claimant is already receiving annuities or ordinary invalidity pension or service invalidity; the applicant can, however, opt for the most favourable treatment. Failure to undergo the legally required medical and specialist controls without good reason cause the applicant to lose all rights to the benefits involved.

217. Mutilates and invalids who have been declared totally disabled, who can neither walk nor look after themselves, who require constant assistance, and who are entitled to inability pension and those who are 100% sight-impaired qualify for the mobility allowance. This benefit is independent of the claimant's earnings and may be paid on top of other benefits, except the accompanying allowance of the social insurance against invalidity.[133]

130. Acts No. 118 of 1971 and No. 33 of 1980.
131. Act No. 188 of 1971.
132. Act No. 289 of 1990. *See also* Constitutional Court Decision No. 106 of 1992.
133. Acts No. 18 of 1980 and No. 508 of 1988. *See also* Act No. 492 of 1991.

Part X. Minimum Income Benefit

Chapter 1. Citizenship Income

218. Act No. 26/2019 introduced, starting from April 2019, the citizenship income (RDC). The RDC is regarded as a fundamental measure of active labour market policy, to combat poverty, inequality and all social exclusion, as well as aimed at favouring the right to work, information, education, training and culture. The RDC finds its instruments in policies aimed at economic support and social inclusion of those at risk of marginalization in society and in employment. According to the law, the RDC constitutes 'the essential level of benefits within the limits of available resources'.

For households composed exclusively of one or more members aged 67 (periodically adapted in relation to increases in life expectancy) or over, the RDC takes the name of Citizenship pension as a measure to combat the poverty of elderly people.

The economic benefit is provided through the RDC Card: a social card with respect to which payments are authorized in relation to the specific needs listed by the law.

The RDC is recognized to families who have, cumulatively, at the time of submitting the application and for the entire duration of the allowance, the following requirements: Italian citizenship, or citizenship of countries belonging to the European Union, or possession by a family member of the right of residence or of permanent residence, or possession by a Non-EU citizens of the EU residence permit for long-term residents; residency in Italy for at least ten years, of which the last two, considered at the time of submitting the application and for the entire duration of the benefit, on a continuous basis; values of the Equivalent economic situation indicator (ISEE), of the real estate assets (different from the dwelling house), of movable property and of the family income, as defined for ISEE purposes, lower than a certain threshold; absence of entitlement to the property of any vehicle registered for the first time in the six months prior to the application, or motor vehicles with a cylinder capacity exceeding 1,600 cc or motorcycles with a capacity greater than 250 cc, first registered in the two years antecedent the application; absence of entitlement of ships and pleasure boats; absence of criminal convictions or precautionary measures for serious crimes.

The RDC is recognized for the period during which the beneficiary is in the expected conditions and, in any case, for a continuous period not exceeding eighteen months. The RDC can be renewed, after suspension of the same for a period of one month before every renewal. The suspension does not operate in the case of Citizenship pension.

The payment of the benefit is conditional on the declaration of immediate availability to work by all the adult members of the family unit and adherence to a personalized project geared both to the reinstatement in a job position and to social inclusion. The project might provide for services for the community, professional retraining, completion of studies, as well as other commitments identified by the competent employment agencies aimed at re-entering the labour market. The GOL programme (Workers Employability Guarantee) also addresses the RDC recipients: this is a PNRR (Recovery and Resilience Plan in the ambit of Next Generation EU) scheme geared to the reintegration into the labour market of the unemployed. The RDC recipients are due to accept at least one out of two adequate job offers. The failure to accept adequate job offers is sanctioned by reducing the benefit of EUR 5.00 a month, except that the performance does not drop below a minimum limit fixed by the law. The non-compliance in the activation of a family member in the search for a job reverberates in the entire family unit.

Chapter 2. Social Allowance

§1. Beneficiaries

219. The social allowance took over from the social pension on 1 January 1996. The social pension, introduced towards the end of the 1960s, was the first universal benefit in Italy, that is, the first to address all the citizens. This benefit, based on Article 38, paragraph 1 of the Constitution, was inspired by criteria of wealth redistribution. The social pension, like the present-day social allowance, was provided as a right. The social allowance was brought in with the Pensions Reform Act No. 335 of 1995. It is run by the Social Assistance and Social Insurance Support Fund at the INPS and is entirely funded by the central government. The amount paid by the social allowance is higher than that paid by social pension, but the requirements for receiving it are stricter. The social allowance is in fact means tested.[134]

220. The first condition to be met when applying for social allowance is Italian citizenship; the applicant must not only be an Italian citizen when the application is made, but also as long as the benefit is paid; if this condition is not met, the benefit is withdrawn. In addition to citizenship, the applicant must reside in Italy since at least ten years. The EU citizens and extra-communitarian people with long-term residence permit are equalized to Italian citizens.[135] Another condition is that the applicant must have 67 years of age. The final requirement is that the applicant has earnings inferior to a certain threshold. If the applicant is married, the spouse's earnings are taken into consideration and the threshold is doubled. However, if the applicant or his/her spouse have earnings, the social allowance will be reduced proportionally. If these thresholds are exceeded the benefit is withdrawn. The following are taken into consideration in the earnings calculations: any sort of net earnings, after taxes and social contributions deductions; maintenance benefits. The following are not taken into consideration: retirement lump-sum payments; any back pay that is differently taxed; the applicant's social allowance; earnings imputed to the claimant's house; one-third of any pension paid under the contribution system.

§2. Amount of the Benefit

221. Social allowance is paid by INPS, in the same way as the general social insurance scheme pensions. The benefit is an annuity, paid for thirteen months. The social allowance is temporarily paid on the basis of the applicant's statements and is then modified according to the official earning declaration for IRPEF purposes presented by the applicant. If the claimant is aged 70 and his/her earnings are below

---

134. Alongside social allowance, the Italian system has another benefit known as the 'integration of pensions up to the minimum'. This benefit, abolished by the 1995 pension reform, is still applied under the retributive system of calculation of pensions. It is a benefit that brings pensions up to the legal minimum. It was dealt with in detail in Part VIII of this study.
135. *See* EC Regulation No. 1247/1992.

certain limits, the social allowance amount is increased. The amount of the benefit is index-related through the same system provided for pensions of workers of the private sector. The benefit, as part of an assistance service, cannot be passed on after death, nor transferred, nor sequestered, nor pawned.

222. The social allowance cannot be cumulated to other social assistance or social insurance benefits paid with continuity by the state or by other public bodies or by a foreign government, nor to war pensions. This clause does not apply when the sum of the other benefits does not reach the amount of the social allowance: in this case, the social allowance is proportionally reduced.

Part XI. Claims and Adjudication

Chapter 1. Claims and Adjudication

§1. The Administrative Process

223. In Italy, disputes in matters of welfare and assistance are administered on two levels. These are the appeals by administrative channels and those by judicial means. The administrative phase is obligatory: the judicial phase, indeed, may not take place if the individual who believes him/herself the damaged party has not made recourse to the administrative bodies of protection. In other words, presentation of the request through administrative channels by the interested party is the *sine qua non* for legal action: in the absence of the former, the request by legal means is rejected because it is deemed 'procedurally inadmissible'.[136] The reason for this is the need to maintain the traditional privilege of the public administration to examine its own actions before being confronted by a legal case. In addition, there has always been an attempt to keep disputes in which the public administration constitutes a party separate from ordinary legal trials, and the subordination of ordinary jurisdiction to prior examination by administrators in this matter is in tune with this policy. In practice, by means of the expectation of an obligatory phase of dispute at the administrative level, a primary control over a welfare measure, conducted with the same criteria as those used for the emanation of the same measure, is assured.

224. The regulation of disputes in matters of social insurance and assistance at the administrative level has never been unitary in our country. Every form of social insurance, indeed, has a particular system for disputes relating to it. In particular, the various attributions, besides being divided among the various forms of insurance, are also divided between the peripheral and central bodies of the different pension organizations, and between different organs, depending on whether the appeal has as its object contributions or welfare payments. A rationalization of the subject was nevertheless brought about by Act No. 533 of 1973, pertaining to lawsuits relating to work and welfare. This law also differentiated legal administrative procedures in matters of welfare and pensions from other administrative procedures. In particular, this law established that any time limit laid down by law for the presentation of an appeal through administrative channels in matters of social insurance

136. Article 443 of the Code of Civil Procedure.

and assistance does not constitute a deadline of forfeiture.[137] In addition, there is a dispensation to the general rule according to which the contents of an appeal limits the subject and the grounds of the re-examination on the part of the judge. This rule lays down that when, during the course of the procedure, a new reason for objection arises that was not originally presented in the appeal, the deciding authority cannot take it into examination: its decision must be based on the grounds outlined in the appeal. So, in the area of social insurance and assistance disputes this rule is not applied. Indeed, the re-examination does not have as its subject simply the elimination of the contested action, but rather the overall re-examination of the decision of the authority that emanated the act that has been objected to. It is thus possible for the body giving judgment also to take into consideration grounds for objection that are new compared with those outlined in the appeal. In technical terms, the Act of 1973 gives expression to this concept by affirming that in administrative procedures regarding disputes in matters of obligatory social insurance and assistance, no consideration is made of errors, preclusions, and expirations that may have occurred.[138] This peculiarity in appeals in the field of social insurance permits greater protection of the interests of the individual lodging an appeal.

§2. The Trial Before an Ordinary Judge

225. Once the administrative procedure is over, the still unsatisfied appellant has the right to make legal representation to the ordinary judge. The presentation of a lawsuit before a judge is subject to a time limit. Trials pertaining to social insurance and assistance are regulated by Act No. 533 of 1973, together with trials pertaining to employment. In particular, for what is of interest here, the disputes to which the law cited above applies are those that arise in the following areas: social insurance, industrial accidents and professional diseases, family benefits, other forms of obligatory social insurance and assistance, social insurance and assistance deriving from collective contracts and agreements, and thus also complementary private pensions.

226. The system dictated by the law of 1973 introduced a special procedure with the main aim of ensuring speedier legal protection than that of the ordinary trial. This was also true in consideration of the interests beyond that of the individual implied in matters of employment and pensions. The procedural model chosen was that of a specific, non-summary procedure, inspired by the requirements of oral testimony, of concentration, and of immediacy. This procedural model was conceived as being very flexible. For example, the addition of new facts during the case is permitted; in an ordinary trial this is not allowed and the judge is limited in his/her decision by what was included in the plaintiff's original appeal. Legal practice has used this possibility with extreme amplitude in authorizing the addition of new facts, even after judgment in the first instance.

137. Article 8, Act No. 533 of 1973.
138. Article 8, Act No. 533 of 1973.

The procedure is characterized in addition by the principle of low-cost; this is a principle that, over the years, unfortunately has been very much mitigated. The proceedings are almost free: only a unified contribution for acts has to be paid. The unsuccessful employee whose earnings are inferior to a fixed ceiling – which, over time, has become however quite low – is exempt from payment of his/her legal costs; neither must he/she pay those of the other party in the case. The employee will, in any case, be expected to pay costs if his/her suit is judged to be reckless and manifestly without foundation. There is not, however, assistance laid down for the payment of legal advice. The only type of aid in this regard comes from the unions, which supply free legal advice to their members.

227. It must be said, however, that in practice even proceedings of this kind are very slow. They are never completed in a single session or hearing, and they can last even several years. This is because the theoretical principles underlying this special procedure are not implemented through specific rules. Moreover, the number of proceedings is very high while the courts are badly understaffed. With a view to limiting the problem of the long duration of trials, a general norm has recently been introduced at the constitutional level which establishes the principle of the reasonable length of a trial; violation of this principle results in equitable compensation.[139]

228. Another obstacle to the certainty of legislation in this area is represented by the complexity and obscurity of social security legislation, which, among other things, is affected by very frequent modifications. This may cause different interpretations of the same provision (which may even result in the withdrawal of social security benefits), an increase in litigation, and a growing complexity of the social security system, which becomes more and more difficult to disentangle, not just for laymen and their lawyers but even for the legislator and the administrators themselves.

§3. The Trial Before the Administrative Judge

229. In Italy, alongside the ordinary judge there is the administrative judge. The administrative judge has competences laid down by law. In particular, he/she has general jurisdiction of legitimacy in any cases in which individuals have legal positions of legitimate interest against the public administration. Legitimate interest is a legal position that is weakened with respect to individual rights. In a case of legitimate interest the individual possesses a claim to treatment that is equitable and in conformity with the law against the public administration which has, on the other hand, discretionary power in the recognition of certain legal situations. The administrative judge also has exclusive jurisdiction in certain matters.

In the field of welfare, regarding measures dealing with unemployment, disputes relating to recognition of ordinary and extraordinary interventions of short-time earning funds are referred to the jurisdiction of the administrative judge. The Court

139. *See* Art. 111 of the Italian Constitution; Art. 2, Act No. 89 of 2001.

of Cassation (*Corte di Cassazione*, the highest Italian Court of Appeal) maintains, indeed, that the public administration enjoys authority and discretionary powers in these matters.[140]

Still, in the area of administrative jurisdiction, disputes in the matter of war pensions, and ordinary and privileged pensions that are owed by the state are entrusted to the audit court (*Corte dei Conti*).

140. Court of Cassation, United Sections, 17 May 1991, No. 5530.

Chapter 2. The Protection of Pension Rights and Contribution Credits

§1. The Protection of Pension Rights

I. The Legal System of Pension Rights

230. Pension rights are considered by Italian Constitution as fundamental rights. As such they are personal, irrevocable, inalienable, non-transmissible, without distraint and with inviolable rights. These rights cannot be curtailed even by the possessor of those rights him/herself. Any possible relinquishment or settlement brought about by the possessors of pension rights is null and void.[141] However, specific dispensations to the general principle of the unalterable nature of these rights exist in particular situations, which are peremptorily laid down. The system ensuring that pension credits are without distraint, for example, has a dispensation in the case of credits for alimony.

It should be remembered here, however, that very often the right to payment is subject to the fulfilment of certain onus on the part of the insured person. One of these is the presentation of a request to the pension authority in order to obtain payment. Presentation of the request to the administrative headquarters constitutes the necessary precondition for any possible judicial application. In the absence of a request to the administrative headquarters, a court action is inadmissible.

231. The right to a pension is not subject to any statute of limitations, both in the public and private sector. In the public sector the absence of time limitation is sanctioned explicitly by a law;[142] in the private sector it is re-affirmed by legal practice which is by now constant. Individual accruals of pensions are, on the other hand, subject to statutes of limitations. The time limit is of five years.[143] Other pension payments have specific time limits. The right to economic benefits for the coverage of industrial injuries and professional diseases is limited to three years from the day of the injury or the onset of the illness. The right to family allowance benefits is cancelled in five years.

232. Alongside these legal time limits there are much more rigid forfeiture deadlines. In particular, the interested party loses the right to take legal action to obtain his/her pension payment that has been tacitly or expressly denied by the pension body after three years, if it is a pension, and after one year for temporary benefit payments. The forfeiture deadline runs from the day on which the right to a claim can be exercised. This deadline has a substantial and not only a procedural nature: once the deadline has passed, indeed, even the right to accruals that were previous to payment is lost. In reality, the statutory time limits often end up being absorbed

141. *See* Arts 2115 and 1966 of the Italian Civil Code.
142. Article 5 of Presidential Decree No. 1092 of 1973.
143. Act No. 211/2011.

by the forfeiture deadlines. These deadlines are obviously favourable time limits for the pension bodies, even if their ratio is officially identified in the economic requirements of legal remedies.

II. The Retained Payments (*Soluti Retentio*)

233. In Italy's legal system, the position of a pensioner who finds him/herself having to repay to the pension body payments received in error, but in good faith, on the basis of a measure that is formally correct but invalid in substance, is protected. Often, indeed, the subject who receives pension payments uses them for spending on basic necessities and might not be able to repay the sums received by him/her in error and unknowingly. In these situations restitution of sums received in error is not asked of the pensioner. This is true both in the case of errors regarding the total amount of payments and in cases of errors regarding the existence of the pension payment itself. This system, known as the *soluti retentio*, applies with certain limits. In general, this system applies only in connection with pensions that are part of general obligatory national social insurance. In particular, in the private sector, the *soluti retentio* applies only in relation to sums paid on the basis of a formal and definitive measure, communicated explicitly to the interested party, invalidated by an error attributable to the pension body. In addition, the undeserved payment must not be due to fraud on the part of the insured person. The collection of undeserved payments does not extend to the surviving relatives of a pensioner.[144]

III. Automatic Revaluation of Pension Credits

234. Pension and welfare credits are subject to automatic monetary revaluation (i.e., they are index-linked). This mechanism allows the credit to be brought back up to its original value. Automatic revaluation means that the judge, in pronouncing judgment ordering payment of pension benefits, must determine, in addition to the legal interest, the greatest potential damages suffered by the insured person in the delay of payment, due to the reduction in real value of the sum owing. Such damages are calculated by making reference to the greater amount from either that of the ISTAT retail price index or that of the legal interest.[145] In the public sector, by contrast, only legal interest is owed.

IV. Measures to Guarantee Effectiveness of Protection

235. Finally, possible cases of specific protection exist in situations in which pension rights are put at risk by non-payment of contributions on the part of the employer. One of the remedies laid down by the legal system is the principle of

144. With reference to payments relating to coverage for industrial accidents and professional diseases, *see* Art. 55, Act No. 88 of 1989; Art. 9, Legislative Decree No. 38/2000.
145. Article 16, para. 6, Act No. 412/1991, as modified by Act No. 296/2006 and Act No. 35/2012.

automatic payment of benefits, which has already been mentioned above. This principle is laid down by Article 2116 of the Civil Code. In compliance with this principle, the benefits to be paid by the obligatory pension and welfare systems are owed to the worker even when the employer has not paid the proper contributions. This principle naturally applies only to the benefit of the employee and does not extend to the self-employed. In addition, the principle in question applies in a complete manner only for social insurance against industrial accidents and occupational diseases. In the case of obligatory social insurance for invalidity, old-age, and survivors, the principle only applies within the time period of limitation of contributions. This means that once the employer's debt of contributions is paid off because of statutory limitation, the worker cannot invoke the principle of automatic payment of benefits. Some years ago, however, this principle was strengthened within the pension system as well.[146] In particular, it has been established that in the case of an employer being subject to executive procedure, the worker can ask the welfare institution that omitted contributions or those already limited be considered as having been paid. The only condition that the legislator has placed on the applicability of the principle in this case is the previous attempt on the part of the employee to enact proceedings against the employer for redress: the principle will be applicable only if the legal proceedings on the part of the employee have a negative outcome.

It must be noted here that the law on pension reform of 1995 unified the limitation term of all contributions to five years. In addition, it must be stated that in the pension field, as a specific dispensation to the general rules, the possibility to regularize contributions in arrears is excluded once the limitation has come into play. This principle, which has the intention of protecting the welfare institutions from unforeseen pension payments, has the effect that once the limitation has come into effect, the contribution position of a worker is definitively prejudiced.

When the principle of automatic payment of benefits cannot be applied, there are two other remedies against the non-payment of contributions by the employer. One of these is precisely the court action for damages against the employer according to Article 2116 of the Italian Civil Code, which has just been mentioned. The prescription period for such an action is ten years; this legal time limit is counted from the moment in which the insured person sees his/her application for pension payment rejected by the pension body, or accepted with inferior conditions to those he would have expected as a result of the irregular or non-payment of contributions on the part of the employer. The credit for the worker's damages is aided by a general lien on the movable goods of the employer. Alternatively, the worker who loses his/her right to benefits payment as a consequence of non-payment of contributions on the part of an employer may make a legal request for the constitution of a lifetime income to be paid by the employer.

146. Article 3, Legislative Decree No. 80 of 1992.

§2. Protection of Contribution Credits

I. Additional Obligations of the Employer

236. The legal system sets out a series of measures aimed at rendering the process of acquisition of financial resources earmarked for the welfare system effectively. Among these, employers' secondary obligations are to be found. In particular, the employer has the duty to report all workers taken on, and the payments made to them; this information is recorded in registers kept by the employer; last, the employer must specify in these records the characteristics of the work activities done. In addition, the pension bodies are given powers of supervision and verification of contributory debts. Secondary obligations are accompanied by civil, administrative, and criminal law sanctions.

Moreover, in order to benefit of contributive benefits and to take part in contracts with the public administration, employers have to obtain the DURC.[147]

II. General Lien on Movable Goods

237. Credits owing to the pension bodies are aided by the general lien on the movable goods of the debtor. Contribution credits, both those to be paid by employers and those owed by the self-employed, enjoy general lien for the entire sum owing; while the credits for secondary sums, such as civil or administrative sanctions and their interest, enjoy general lien limited to 50%.

III. Prescription of Contribution Credits

238. The system for statutory limitation of contributory credits has been subject to numerous legislative interventions. The subject is very delicate. On the one hand, there are the interests of the pension bodies to have wide time periods of prescription that might help in the collection of contributions. On the other hand, there are the interests of employers not to experience verifications and objections by the pension bodies that relate to events that date back in time. The pension reform legislation of 1995 has allowed the interests of employers to prevail as well as that of containing the contributions burden, by unifying the statutory time limits of all obligatory welfare contributions to five years.[148] It should be remembered here that the lapsing of statutory time limits has very significant effects on the voluntary payment of forfeited contributions. Indeed, a norm of 1936,[149] as a special dispensation to common law, excludes the possibility of effecting payments to regularize contributions in arrears, once the statutory time limit has run out, for all insurance

147. Article 1, para. 1175, Act No. 296/2006.
148. Act No. 335 of 1995.
149. Article 55, Royal Law Decree No. 1827 of 1935.

schemes managed by INPS. The 1995 reform generalized this principle with the declared aim of insulating the pension bodies from heavy and unexpected financial responsibilities.

IV. Powers of the Watchdog Organizations of the Pension Bodies

239. Special powers have been conferred on both the Employment Ministry and the pension bodies to aid them in the collection of contributory credit.

Law Decree No. 149/2015, however, has established an agency called National Work Inspectorate, with local offices, in order to integrate the local inspector's sections of the Employment Ministry, of INAIL and INPS and, over time, to replace them.

In the meantime, the verification organizations of pension bodies have powers of supervision and notice. These prerogatives are given practical significance in the power of inspection and access to all company sites, with the intention of verification of the orderliness of payments and the investigation of possible violations of welfare regulations. During the course of such inspections the pension bodies may take all necessary information from employers, employees, and unions present in the company that is relevant to the existence and nature of working relationships, to payments owed, and to contributory obligations. This information is then recorded in the appropriate minutes. These minutes must then be communicated to the company. Communication must also take place in cases in which the regular status of the contribution position of the employer is called into question. The law of pension reform of 1995 established that, once minutes have been produced, it is no longer possible to charge the employer with non-payments relative to periods prior to the date of the emission of those minutes. The inspection organizations of the pension bodies also have the power of notification of the infringements investigated. This power must be used within ninety days of the investigation (three-hundred and sixty days for people resident abroad); otherwise, the relative sanction will not apply. The inspection organizations, finally, have the power of sequestration of things constituting proof of the administrative contravention.

The contributory credits of pension bodies may be drawn by means of registration in assessment lists, have a specific collection procedure[150] and may be conceded *en masse* for a valuable consideration to joint-stock companies founded for the precise purpose, which take charge of the collection of the credits. This has the intention of making collection quicker.

V. Sanctions Laid Down for Non-payment of Contributions

240. Non-fulfilment in the payment of contributions on the part of the employer is punished with civil sanctions. It is to be remembered here that the employer is responsible for the process of payment not only of contributions due from him/her, but also of those owing from the employee. In the event of delayed payment or

150. Article 30, Act No. 122/2010.

omission of contributions on the part of the employer, a civil law sanction is automatically applied. This has the nature of an additional obligation in respect to the principal contributory obligation and represents a compensation for damages caused to the pension body. The civil law sanction increases every year up to a maximum ceiling, which is fixed between 30% and 40% of unpaid or delayed contributions, depending on each case; once the sanctions have reached the maximum total without the employer's contribution position being put right, legal interest is applied to the total sum of the principal contributory obligation. For some years, however, the legislator has granted employers who arrange for the regularization of their contribution position the remission of civil law sanctions. The measure of an amnesty of this kind, which is debatable from the point of view of the principles and values of the legal system, has always been dictated by the need to recoup the huge sums of payments evaded by companies. In addition, the power to reduce sanctions to the legal interest rate has been granted to the pension bodies, in the presence of special reasons justifying non-payment.[151] One of these extenuating circumstances has been identified in the existence of legal disputes over a given matter. It is relevant to note here that the legal time limit for the prescription of contributions is five years.

Administrative law sanctions are also laid down for the violation of obligations that are additional to the obligation to contribution. Such is, for example, the obligation of having to supply pension bodies with the elements necessary for the calculation of contributions.

Instead the following are punishable by criminal law: omissions or falsehoods in obligatory registrations or reports, when these have the consequence of omission of payment of a certain sum of contributions laid down by law; the non-payment of welfare deductions made by the employer on employees' pay, for sums over EUR 10,000 (a similar sanction is applied to the commissioners as regards self-employment).[152]

VI. The Unnecessary Payment of Contributions

241. Unnecessary payment happens when an employer pays contributions that are not owing to the pension body. In these cases, usually, the individual who has paid contributions that are not owing has the right to have the sum back. The pension body is obliged to add to the sum unnecessarily received the greater amount from either that of legal interest or that of monetary revaluation, without the employer having to prove the damages really suffered. In the case in which restitution of contribution payments unnecessarily made occurs, these naturally are not taken into consideration in calculation of the right to, or amount of, welfare payments subsequently paid out. However, the law lays down that those contributions for which the assessment of unnecessary payment occurs later than five years from the date of payment become the property of the pension body. The rule applies only where there is a valid welfare obligation in any case.

151. Article 116, Act No. 388/2000.
152. Article 39, Act No. 183/2010.

VII. Legal Measures for Facilitation in the Collection of Contributory Credit

242. Protection of the contribution credits of the welfare institutions includes also privileged proceeding instruments. One of these consists of the attribution of the value of executive authority to the statements of the directors of the territorial head offices that collect contributory credits. The value of executive authority is in the same way attributed to the reports, declarations, and certificates of recognition of debt made by employers obliged to make payment of contributions. Attribution of the value of executive authority means that the distraint of the goods of the non-paying contributor may be requested directly, without making formal application to a judge to obtain such a proceeding. Another instrument available to the welfare bodies is the injunction. This is an act with the authority to command payment, which may be formulated by the same welfare body without the need for recourse to a judge. The injunction may be used for the collection of contribution credits and of sanctions. Another procedural aid for pension bodies is represented by the fact that disputes in matters of contributions are attributed to the territorial competence of the judge of the place in which the office of the welfare institution is to be found. Last, judgments on the subject of contributions have provisional executive efficacy; which is to say that they are executive even if they are not yet definitive.

VIII. Actions of Substitution and Recourse of the Pension Bodies

243. Actions of recourse and substitution may be carried out by pension bodies against third parties responsible for damages caused to insured people and covered by welfare benefits. In other words, when welfare services are rendered necessary by illegal action by a third party, the pension bodies are authorized to obtain compensation from the third party responsible for the illegal behaviour. For example, INAIL (the state body providing benefits to people injured at work) may bring an action against the employer criminally responsible for an industrial accident or an occupational disease to recoup the sums paid to the insured worker according to his/her rights to welfare payments (action for recourse). INPS (National Social Welfare Institute) may act in the place of the insured person against the person or company responsible for an infirmity caused to him/her; INAIL and the NHS may do the same thing in relation to payments made to their own insured individuals or clients (action of substitution).

Selected Bibliography

Case Reports

Foro Italiano (Bologna, Zanichelli).
Lavoro e Previdenza Oggi (Rome, LPO).
Repertorio del Foro Italiano (Bologna, Zanichelli).
Rivista del Diritto della Sicurezza Sociale (Bologna, Il Mulino).
Rivista Giuridica del Lavoro (Rome, Ediesse).
Rivista degli Infortuni e delle Malattie Professionali (Rome, INAIL).
Rivista Italiana di Diritto del Lavoro (Milan, Giuffré).

Texts

Ales, A., et al. *Diritto della sicurezza sociale.* Milan: Giuffrè, 2021.
Alibrandi, G. *Infortuni sul lavoro e malattie professionali.* Milan: Giuffrè, 1979.
Avio, A. *Vecchiaia e lavoro. Tra solidarietà e corrispettività.* Rome: Ediesse, 2008.
Balandi, G. G. *Tutela del reddito e mercato del lavoro nell'ordinamento italiano.* Milan: Giuffrè, 1984.
Ballestrero, M. V. *Cassa integrazione guadagni e contratto di lavoro.* Milan: Angeli, 1984.
Bessone, M. *Previdenza complementare.* Turin: Giappichelli, 2000.
Bottari, C. *Tutela dela salute e organizzazione sanitária.* Turin: Giappichelli, 2011.
Bozzao, P. *La tutela previdenziale del lavoro discontinuo.* Turin: Giappichelli, 2005.
Bronzini, G. *Il reddito di cittadinanza.* Turin: Edizioni Gruppo Abele, 2011.
Carnelutti, F. *Infortuni sul lavoro.* Rome: Athenaeum, I e II, 1913–1914.
Casillo, R. *La pensione di vecchiaia. Un diritto in trasformazione.* Naples: ESI, 2016.
Cinelli, M. *Diritto della previdenza sociale.* Turin: Giappichelli, 2022.
Cinelli, M. *Il rapporto previdenziale.* Turin: Giappichelli, 2007.
Cinelli, M. *La tutela del lavoratore contro la disoccupazione.* Milan: Angeli, 1982.
Cinelli, M. & Giubboni, S. *Cittadinanza, lavoro, diritti sociali. Percorsi nazionali e europei.* Turin: Giappichelli, 2014.
Cinelli, M. & Giubboni, S. *Il diritto della sicurezza sociale in trasformazione.* Turin: Giappichelli, 2005.
De Matteis, A. *Infortuni sul lavoro e malattie professionali.* Milan: Giuffrè, 2016.
Del Punta, R. & D. Gottardi. *I nuovi congedi.* Milan: Il Sole 24 ore, 2001.
De Matteis, A. & S. Giubboni. *Infortuni sul lavoro e malattie professionali.* Milan: Giuffrè, 2005.

Selected Bibliography

Gaeta, L. *Infortuni sul lavoro e responsabilità civile. Alle origini del diritto del lavoro.* Naples: ESI, 1986.
Lagala, C. *La previdenza sociale tra mutualità e socialità.* Bari: Cacucci, 2001.
Mastrangeli, F. D. & C. A. Nicolini. *La contribuzione previdenziale.* Turin: Utet, 1997.
Olivelli, P. *La Costituzione e la sicurezza sociale.* Milan: Giuffrè, 1988.
Persiani, M. *Il sistema giuridico della previdenza sociale.* Padua: Cedam, 1960.
Persiani, M. *Diritto della previdenza sociale.* Padua: Cedam, 2007.
Persiani, M. *Previdenza complementare.* Padua: Cedam, 2008.
Persiani, M. & D'Onghia, M. *Diritto della previdenza sociale.* Turin: Giappichelli, 2022.
Pessi, R. *La previdenza complementare.* Padua: Cedam, 1999.
Pessi, R. *Lezioni di diritto della previdenza sociale.* Padua: Cedam, 2016.
Renga, S. *Mercato del lavoro e diritto.* Milan: Angeli, 1996.
Renga, S. *La tutela sociale dei lavori.* Turin: Giappichelli, 2006.
Renga, S. *Bilateralità e sostegno del reddito tra autonomia e eteronomia.* Padua: Cedam, 2013.
Sciarra, S. (ed.). *Solidarietà, mercato e concorrenza nel* welfare *italiano.* Bologna: Il Mulino, 2007.

Articles

'Il completamento della riforma pensionistica'. *Lavoro e diritto* (2008): 606.
'La nuova disciplina della previdenza complementare' (d.leg. 5 dicembre 2005 n. 252), ed. Tursi, A. *Nuove leggi civili commentate* (2007): 535.
Andreoni, A. 'Inabilità'. *Digesto Civile, sezione commerciale* (1991).
Avio, A. 'Vecchiaia nel diritto della sicurezza sociale'. *Digesto Civile, sezione commerciale* (1999).
Balandi, G.G. 'Sicurezza sociale'. *Digesto Civile, sezione commerciale* (1996).
Balandi, G.G. 'Le malattie professionali: una quadro normativo in evoluzione'. *Rivista italiana di diritto del lavoro* I (1989): 235.
Balandi, G.G. 'Assicurazione sociale'. *Digesto Civile, sezione commerciale* (1987).
Balandi, G.G. 'Per una definizione del diritto della previdenza sociale'. *Politica del diritto* (1984): 576.
Balandi, G.G. 'Un caso di archeologia giuridica: ciò che resta oggi del rischio professionale'. *Rivista giuridica del lavoro* III (1976): 98.
Bozzao, P. 'La protezione sociale della famiglia'. *Lavoro e diritto* (2001): 55.
Bozzao, P. 'Gli ammortizzatori social nel sistema del Jobs act: una visione d'insieme'. *Diritti Lavori Mercati* (2015): 519.
Castronovo, C. 'Danno alla salute e infortuni. La Corte costituzionale e i diritti secondi'. *Foro Italiano* I (1995): 84.
Cinelli, M. 'La riforma dele pensioni del governo tecnico'. *Rivista italiana di diritto del lavoro* (2012):385.
Ciocca, G. 'Il sistema previdenziale ed il federalismo'. *Argomenti di diritto del lavoro* (2003): 739.
Commentario della Costituzione cured by G. Branca (Zanichelli – Il Foro italiano, Bologna and Rome 1979), sub-Article 38.
Gottardi, D. 'Lavoro di cura. Spunti di riflessione'. *Lavoro e diritto* (2001): 121.

Nicolini, C.A. 'La cassa integrazione guadagni'. *Commentario breve dela reforma Jobs act* (Cedam, Padova 2016): 181.
Mengoni, L. 'La tutela dei lavoratori contro la disoccupazione nel diritto italiano'. *La tutela dei lavoratori contro la disoccupazione* (Luxemburg, 1961).
Proia, G. 'Sussidiarietà e previdenza'. *Argomenti di diritto del lavoro* (2006): 1567.
Renga, S. 'Post fata resurgo: la rivincita del principio assicurativo nella tutela dela disoccupazione'. *Lavoro e Diritto* (2015): 77.
Sandulli, P. 'Riforma pensionistica e previdenza integrativa'. *Diritto del lavoro e relazioni industriali* (1991): 256.
Sandulli, P. 'Crisi ed evoluzione del sistema previdenziale italiano'. *Diritto del lavoro* I (1988): 216.
Sandulli, P. 'L'assicurazione infortuni sul lavoro in un ventennio di evoluzione legislativa del sistema previdenziale'. *Rivista infortuni e malattie professionali* I (1985): 17.
Sandulli, P. 'La ridefinizione dell'assetto normativo in tema di assicurazione contro gli infortuni sul lavoro e le malattie professionali'. *Rivista infortuni e malattie professionali* I (1999): 643.
Sandulli, P. 'Il sistema pensionistico tra una manovra e l'altra. Prime riflessioni sulla legge n. 214 del 2011'. *Rivista di diritto dela sicurezza sociale* (2012): 1.
Santoro Passarelli, F. 'Rischio e bisogno nella previdenza sociale'. *Rivista italiana di previdenza sociale* (1948): 177.
Tullini, P. 'Salute nel diritto della sicurezza sociale'. *Digesto Civile, sezione commerciale* (1996).

Selected Bibliography

Index

The numbers here refer to paragraph numbers.

Index

Index

www.ingramcontent.com/pod-product-compliance
Ingram Content Group UK Ltd.
Pitfield, Milton Keynes, MK11 3LW, UK
UKHW020146290926
15471UKWH00004B/724

9 789403 516769